Table of Contents

About the Authors

Clinton Keith is a Certified Scrum Trainer and agile coach who, over the course of 30 years, has gone from programming avionics for advanced fighter jets and underwater robots to overseeing programming for hit video game titles such as Midtown Madness and Midnight Club. Clint has been a programmer, project director, CTO, and director of product development at several studios.

He is the author of "Agile Game Development with Scrum" published in May 2010. Since then he has coached and trained at over 100 companies that combine creative and technical visions into their products, such as Apple and ILM.

Grant Shonkwiler first started making games when he was 12 years old, starting with modding and programming. Since then he has filled many different roles in technology industries; programmer, lead designer, technical producer and producer. His career has taken him from casual games at Megatouch Games, to AAA shooters at id Software and to Epic Games to work on Fortnite. Grant has published over 75 technology and game products.

Grant is currently a Production Consultant & Contractor working with all types of technology teams to create great products! Grant also enjoys building communities within the industry working with the IGDA and the GameDevDrinkup. On the weekends you can find Grant on a Rugby Pitch or jumping out of perfectly good airplanes.

Acknowledgements

Clinton Keith

First and foremost, I thank Grant for his hard work and creativity. Second, I'd like to thank who has contributed their practices and ideas to this book (listed in the credits section).

Years ago, as the Chief Technical Officer for a studio, I gathered the eight most talented developers from across our large studio into single team hoping it would become an extremely productive group. The reality was the opposite. They barely accomplished anything of value, spending much of their time arguing about who was right and were unable to come to a decision and focus on a single goal. This taught me important lessons about what a great creative team needs and guided me onto a path of coaching teams and companies on the human side of the problem.

This led to the adoption of many of the practices in this book, which focus on consensus, collaboration and facilitation.

Grant Shonkwiler

I would like to thank all of the amazing producers and leaders who I've worked with throughout my career, your feedback and ideas are living in these pages. I want to thank everyone who contributed to the book, especially our fearless leader Clinton. I want to thank my family for always supporting me, especially my wife. I want to thank all of the people who have supported me and offered me a place to stay on my travels, a special thanks to the Barcroft family.

Introduction

This book got its start in the game development industry. When we tell people that, sometimes they say "video game…like the ones my kids play?" "Yes", we tell them. "Video games that come from the industry that passed the movie industry in revenues over a decade ago". "Video games, like the ones that can take over a thousand developer-years to make and can sell tens of millions of copies for $60 apiece."

Agile practices have created amazing opportunities and challenges to the video game industry. A "cross-discipline" team of artists, musicians and programmers" can be a bit more challenging than a so-called cross-discipline team of programmers. This challenge is becoming more common with the infusion of code in almost every type of product being made. Thermostats aren't simply a mechanical dial anymore. They have beautiful user interfaces and integrate with a host of online services that react to your preferences and even your physical presence. As a result, thermostat developers have to explore how designers, artists and programmers collaborate iteratively to create the best products.

Just as the iPod disrupted the music industry, creative innovation will revolutionize many other areas of life. The challenge in doing that is finding the synthesis of different perspectives to create a sum that's greater than its parts. That is the vision for the practices within this book.

Agile Tools?

Developers always ask "we're having problems doing X with methodology Y, what should we do?". My first answer is "What have you tried?", because the best solutions usually come from the people doing the work and experimenting with new practices, not following so-called best practices.

We're avoiding that phrase "best practices" here because "best" implies there are no better. Practices will always change as do our users, technology and markets. So, consider this book to be a collection of experiments that have provided useful results to some game developers. Some will work for you, others won't.

What makes a practice "advanced"?

While collecting these practices, we've established some criteria that are common among them all:

   Experimental - Expressed as something we are doing to solve a specific problem. If it doesn't solve it, we stop doing it. Implemented with the idea that it will be eliminated or someday replaced with something better (e. g. daily scrum)

Incremental - Not so large that we don't see the benefit, at least in an iteration or release cycle of a few months. They can be validated quickly

Flexible – Not too specific so as to be adaptable to differing needs

Collaborative - Not imposed. Demonstrates consideration, and respect.

Radiative - Visible. Creates transparency. There is sometimes an electronic solution, but they are only recommended for distributed teams

How to Use This Book

This book wasn't written to be read from cover-to-cover. It's meant to be a toolbox of practices to experiment with when you want to improve daily teamwork, how disciplines communicate, how projects manage risk, ways to organize workspaces or to get the most out of your iterations.

The Practice Categories

Daily Teamwork
Practices that teams use to improve daily productivity.

Development Culture
Practices to support improved development methods across all teams.

Facilitation Methods
General practices that coaches and leaders use to facilitate better collaboration and communication.

Individual Growth
Practices that help individuals grow personally and professionally.

Iteration Improvement
Practices which improve the flow of an iteration and reduce its overhead.

Project Management
Practices and approaches for guiding progress on the long-term goals of the product.

Company Improvements
Practices for improving how companies support developers.

Team Culture
Practices that improve team bonding and communication.

Section 1 - Daily Teamwork

Add a Fourth Daily Question

Add a fourth daily question that gets to the heart of the iteration goal

The starting script for the daily stand-up is to have every developer answer three questions:
What have you done since we last met?
What are you working on next?
What is getting in your way?

These questions are not fixed rules and are often modified and supplemented by the team to make the meeting more effective. One example of this is to ask a fourth question about the team's view on the progress of the iteration.

The Practice
The fourth daily question can take many forms and is usually directed at the entire team once all the developers have answered the first three questions or have gone through their individual updates. The question is posed mainly to determine everyone's the level of optimism and commitment to achieving the iteration goal. Sometimes the team as a whole can start to feel a little pessimistic about the iteration and this question will help to address any possible issues as early as possible. One way to do this is to conduct a Roman vote. Ask the team *"Are we going to achieve our iteration goal?"* On the count of three, they either vote thumbs up (if they believe they will achieve it) or thumbs down (if they believe they won't).

Tips
- Ask the question and practice the silent count
- If the consensus is negative, don't address it in the stand-up, instead take it up with the right parties by talking to individuals or calling a meeting between them and the product owner.

Related Practices
The Silent Count
Team Health

Fix Bugs Now

Fix bugs in the iteration instead of never

There is a tendency in development to just keep pushing bugs off forever. When you are in the middle of an iteration and bugs are found the team may say, "We will fix this later." If it doesn't get fixed, it ends up getting pushed to the next iteration, then the next etc. So, instead of doing this it is important to separate bugs that are found into buckets.

The Practice
- When bugs come in they should be triaged by a PM.
- If a bug is valid and needs to be fixed it should be given a priority and assigned to a bucket.
- Bugs go into a few buckets:
- Current Iteration - Must be fixed this iteration
- Current Release - Must be fixed before going live
- Never - Not important and won't be fixed but do keep track
- At the beginning of the next iteration look at the bugs in Current Release and decide if they need to be fixed.
- QA should regularly review the bugs in the Never bucket to see if they might have been fixed with new code/features.

Tips
- Bugs that require a lot of work to fix should be turned into stories for future iterations.
- Make sure that QA still knows they should put in every bug they find, even if similar bugs are going into the Never bucket.
- Once a release has happened, have a PM go through the Never bucket and see if anything might be relevant now.

The Silent Count

Help your team solve problems on their own

Description
A good practice for coaches and leaders is to ask questions - and to wait for the answer, even if they might know the answer. The practice is to silently count to 10 after you have asked the question. Don't be surprised if it takes 6-7 seconds before someone responds. Long silences can be uncomfortable for a developer who may know the answer but is just a bit shy to speak up. If you have counted to 10 seconds and no one has spoken up, asking a bridge question can make it easier to get a response to your question.

Example
Coach: "Are we on track to hit our iteration goal this week?"
Silent count to 10.
Coach: "OK, are there any things that you might be concerned about?"
After a few seconds a developer speaks up: "I'm not sure I'm creating the right classes for this problem".
Another developer speaks up: "I can sit with you after the meeting and go over what we need".

Tips
Creating a pattern of problem solving among developers without direct management supervision will give you one of the greatest benefits of self-organization. Having eight people solving 90% of the problems is a lot more efficient and effective than you doing it on your own.

Talk to the Board

Increase team engagement with a focus on getting things done

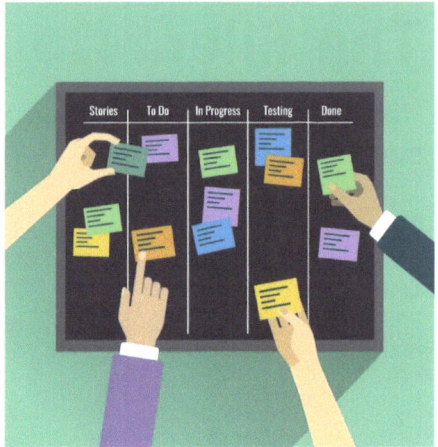

If the team is generally quiet when asked the three questions during the daily stand-up, encourage them to talk to the board instead.

The Practice

This practice requires that the iteration goal, including the collection of product backlog items (PBIs) the team committed to at the start of the iteration, are on the iteration task board. They are usually placed on the left column and are ordered with the highest priority at the top and the lowest at the bottom. The iteration backlog (tasks, etc.) are placed in rows aligning with the PBIs that require them. The Scrum Master, or coach, will go to the board and starting at the highest priority PBI with unfinished work associated with it (tasks in the "not started" or "in progress" columns) ask the team about what needs to be done to complete that PBI. Practice a silent count and if no one speaks up, ask if there are any blockers or impediments that are hindering their progress. Remind the team that higher priority PBIs should ideally take precedence over lower priority PBIs.

Benefits

- Some people will speak up more when facing a board than other team members.
- Focuses the team on finishing PBIs over finishing tasks.
- Highlights impediments more quickly.

Related Practices

The Silent Count

Section 2 - Development Culture

Automate QA

Find something that QA does that can be automated

QA can become overwhelmed with many rote regression testing duties to the point where it can take days or weeks to verify a build. This delay can impact the pace of sharing improvements with the entire team.

The Practice
Based on how QA is testing the product, find a root cause of what they are testing for, *where test automation can be used to expose those problems instead*. Do this on a regular basis with the goal of migrating as much testing to automation as possible.

Tips
- Try to find new ways to add some minimal automation every iteration.
- Speed these tests up and create an order of them running so the most likely problem areas are tested first. The goal is to increase the rate of iteration.
- This will likely create the need to add test servers so be prepared to budget for this.

Examples
Instead of having testers load every widget to test load times and smoke-test the widget, automate the process.
Run smoke tests on as many target platforms as possible with automated scripts

Beachhead a New Practice

Let a single team test a major practice change first

Most practice improvements are small and incremental, but sometimes bigger, more risky leaps are what is needed. It's even riskier when you ask the entire company to make the change at once. Examples of such changes could be:

- Reseating teams into an open cross-discipline space
- Adopting unit testing and continuous integration
- Pairing on all or most of the work
- Swapping out a major part of a production pipeline

The Practice
The approach to beachheading practices for development is the same. The team will adopt the practice for one or more iterations with the following goals:

- Determining whether the practice is beneficial for development
- Finding out if it is a good fit for the company culture
- If possible, determining what changes are required to meet the two previous goals

An existing team can be asked to beach-head a practice or one can be formed for that purpose. The advantage of asking an existing team is that they are used to working together and will be better able to assess if a new practice is beneficial. A newly formed team may allow you to "cherry-pick" a group that might be more enthusiastic about trying a radically different practice (we used this approach in adopting Test-Driven Development practices).

Before the team starts, establish some goals or metrics to evaluate the experiment. For example, if the team is beach-heading a new pipeline, it should be easy to measure the throughput of the completed items.

Tips
- If the practice is a good fit and is beneficial, the beach-head team can coach or encourage other teams as the practice is rolled out. Peers promoting a practice is a great way to put people at ease.

Blessed Build Indicator

Let every developer know, at a glance, how stable the current build is

Should I grab the latest changes? Will they break the build? These are questions that will cause developers to pause before they grab the latest build. These questions result in them delaying their own commits which usually means more changes, increasing the chance that they will break the build.

A good practice that will help to avoid this is implementing a small tool and a testing policy that allows developers to find the most recent build that has been **blessed** (has been tested to the extent that it will function with acceptable performance). The tool allows developers to access the status of the most recent build and to grab the latest blessed build (and understand that it hasn't been fully tested yet).

The Practice
The practice has two major parts. The first is a program that runs on every development machine and has a status indicator on the taskbar. This is usually green when the latest build is blessed, yellow when it is in test mode and red when a fatal error is found. When a developer wants to grab a build, they click on the taskbar icon and a window pops up showing the recent history of builds and their status. They can then select any of the builds and download them or view a report. A build consists of the executable as well as content packages.

The second part is the policy for testing. Initially, this policy involves manually testing builds on the target platform. This will catch a certain percentage of broken builds, but not all of them. Over time, more test automation is added and the definition of "blessed" improves.

References
This book describes more of the test automation.
CreativeAgilityTools.com/Blessed

Form Guilds

Form communities of interest that can foster communication beyond team boundaries

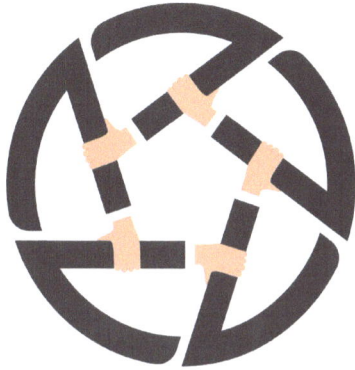

Guilds, communities of practice, orthogonal teams, etc. have been used in addition to cross-functional teams to share and grow expertise with a specific domain.

The Practice
Guilds can form at any time and last as long as needed. They form around a "coordinator" role that, like a Scrum Master, facilitates their purpose. The guild will meet on a regular basis (daily, weekly, etc.) as needed to share the challenges and knowledge centered around their specialization.

Tips
- Don't create a backlog of work for the guilds, but members can jump over to another member's team to help out from time-to-time
- Socialize a guild from time-to-time with events like Pizza Wednesday
- Leverage tools, like Slack, that can help members communicate regularly
- Allow for different levels of participation based on the level of interest and available time
- Explore ways to evolve the purpose of the guild over time. For example, engineers can begin by addressing issues of debt and progress over time to other areas that require attention like architecture or R&D

Examples of Guilds
- Artists who gather to discuss the improvement of tools and methods
- Scrum Masters who share coaching and team practice improvements
- Network security engineers

Related practices
- Pizza Wednesday

Pair Problem Solve

Pair up with another developer and solve a development problem that's slowing one or both of you down

One of the best tools in improving productivity is not trying to speed up what you make, but remove those things that are slowing you down. However, many times the thing slowing you down is out of your control. A dependency that you don't own or a tool that you can't change is often the culprit. Pairing up with someone who can solve that problem is a good solution.

The Practice

As developers work, they encounter problems that they cannot solve. When these problems occur, they fill out a pair problem card. The card contains the following information:

1. Problem description and the name of the developer reporting the problem
2. How much time it costs you to resolve the problem to create a work around.
3. How often it occurs (# of times per week).
4. The discipline you would like to pair with to solve the problem.

These cards form a "pair problem backlog" that is placed in order depending on the answers in #2 and #3.

On a regular basis, the teams hold a matchmaking event where they pick an item from the ordered backlog and pair up. The person that wrote the problem becomes its "customer" of the solution. The other is the "solver". The two work together to solve the problem and remove it from the backlog if it solves the customer's problem. Otherwise it is left on the backlog unsolved.

Tips
- Hold these at a regular cadence. Once a week or sprint works.
- It is effective to time-box the pairing.
- Alternate people's roles as customers and solvers each time.
- Coach the pairs and emphasize that this is a collaborative problem solving effort that requires compromise at times. The customer is not the "boss."

Reduce Integration Time

Explore ways to reduce the overhead on integrating change into your builds

The larger the teams are, the more likelihood there is for overhead to exist when it comes to integrating change into a common build. A continuous effort should be made to reduce that overhead and the time required between making changes and getting them out to the team.

The Practice
This practice is a meta practice of related ones that can be built using a metric of time that can result in more effective development. Start by creating some rough metrics regarding the average time it takes to share changes across the team. Often that time equals the duration of an iteration (e. g. two weeks) because teams only integrate near the end of an iteration.

As you add automation, you can introduce more accurate metrics that show how long it takes for a change to make it into the main branch or a good build. Find ways to reduce that time by improving other practices.

Related Practices
Automate testing
Automate QA
Build Monkey
Blessed build indicator

Rename Scrum Terms

Scrum is meant to be adapted.
Don't let the terms hold you back

Scrum is a starting framework or a script for teams to create and continually improve their product making practices. A lot of teams struggle with adopting Scrum because they view it as a fixed process. This view is reinforced by thousands of articles and dozens of books and it puts blinders on the real goal, which is to own an agile process that works best for your company. *The best adoption of Scrum by companies ends up morphing into something unique.*

Alternatively, teams may find discomfort in some of the roles and practices and rename or eliminate them. Unfortunately, this risks destroying the potential benefit of agile. For example, they may combine the Scrum Master and Product Owner roles because they have Project Managers, or they may avoid forming cross-discipline teams because their company culture resists it. Changes must be made carefully and should reinforce the principles and values of agile and scrum to fully benefit from them.

Examples
Here are some typical renaming of roles, meetings and artifacts
- Scrum Master – Team Coach
- Product Owner - Execution Owner
- Scrum Team - Squad or Strike Team
- Daily Scrum - Daily Standup or Huddle
- Sprint - Iteration

Tips
- When initially adopting Scrum, stick with the Scrum terms from the book until the team is used to them. Think of the Karate Kid waxing Mr. Miyagi's cars; he had to build muscle memory first.
- Train Scrum Masters to understand the principles and values of Scrum well so they can guide the team through changes more easily and effectively.
- Hire an experienced agile coach for a few months to help with guiding the teams.

Scrumble!

Stop what you're making and *fix how you're making it*

Just like cooking a meal in a kitchen filled with dirty pots, pans and utensils, implementing new features without cleaning up the debt of past features will only frustrate you and slow down progress. Sometimes, what is needed is to stop what we're doing, clean up and implement better ways of working.

The Practice

A Scrumble is a break from implementing new features and shifting the focus on bringing the quality of the code and test base up to a sustainable level. It's also a time to examine team and organizational plans and practices such as:

- How branching, merging and integration overhead can be reduced
- How team interdependencies are managed
- How the product backlog is ordered and decomposed before iteration planning
- How the iteration plan is composed and managed
- How testing is conducted and the role of QA

Tips

- Have the duration of the Scrumble decided by the team and product owner ahead of time, or on a day-to-day basis depending on progress.
- Capture practice changes as a list of start, stop and continue actions that are posted where they can be seen by everyone.
- Have the product owner participate in these decisions and agree to abide by them.

The Review Bazaar

For large teams, create an opportunity for the whole group to see what other teams are doing

For large groups that are making a product, a review of the integrated changes made at each iteration in one demo is beneficial. The downside is that there is less exposure to the details of what each team is doing. Occasionally, giving the entire group a chance to get a detailed view of what other teams are doing can give them new insights into the big picture and also reinforce cross-team collaboration.

A review bazaar is a good approach for multi-team reviews.

The Practice
The review bazaar is held instead of an integrated build review usually in the middle of a release. This is where there is likely to be more divergence of mechanics or epics in various stages of progress. The bazaar is ideally held in a single open space with a table running the product for each team. One or more representatives from each team mans the table and everyone else has a chance to walk around, view the builds and ask questions.

Tips
- Review bazaars are also useful for multi-product reviews.
- It is useful for the stakeholders to converge after the bazaar to discuss what they've seen.
- You can hold the bazaar where the teams sit.

Related Practices
The Sprint Day

References
less.works

Viking Points

Incentivize inter-team collaboration

Compartmentalizing teams too much can lead to one team being weighed down with problems while other teams have too little to do. The following practice will encourage teams who have less work to do to help other teams who require assistance.

The Practice
The Viking point is an award given to people helping other teams fix their issues and is represented by a badge or token with a Viking related icon.

Tips
- Viking points can be traded between teams.
- Viking points can be considered as IOU's for future help.
- Some Viking points can be more rare than other ones - creating an incentive to collect more.

Wednesday Pizza Topic

A social event to grow
skills and learn

Growing knowledge and skills should be an essential part of being a
developer. Unfortunately, the pace and urgency of work can make that
growth less of a priority. A great practice is to set aside time for
learning. Sometimes it can be done for the cost of several pizzas.

The Practice
Wednesday Pizza Topic is a practice where a developer presents a
topic to a group of developers every Wednesday night, over pizza (and
beer, if allowed). The format can be whatever the presenter wants, but
interactivity and demonstration are always encouraged. The only
overhead is to have someone facilitate the practice by:
- Scheduling the space
- Organizing and promoting the future presentations
- Ordering the pizza

Tips
- Sessions don't have to be on Wednesdays or after work.
  Lunch sessions work too.
- We found Wednesday to be the best day because it breaks up
  the week and more people can attend during this less busy
  time.
- Sessions can be focused on a single discipline such as
  technical topics for programmers or art topics for artists, or
  cross-discipline topics which are excellent.
- They don't have to directly apply to development. A designer
  who had a film background ran popular sessions where he
  analyzed popular films.

Section 3 - Facilitation Methods

Actively Listen

Communication techniques that focus on actually hearing what people are saying instead of waiting for our chance to speak

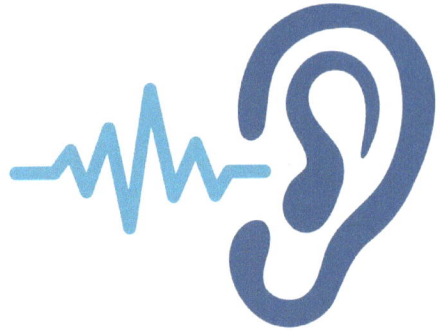

The Practice
The practice of active listening is merely a set of techniques that you can practice to achieve higher levels of comprehension when communicating with others.

Stay focused on what they are saying. Avoid distractions like coming up with the quickest possible answer and waiting to tell them about it. Also, do your best to avoid judgement.

Ask relevant questions - Use **Powerful Questions** that are relevant to what they are saying to elicit more.

Allow for silence. Don't jump in when there is a pause. Practice a **Silent Count** and then ask them a prompting question like "what else…?"

Paraphrase or mirror key phrases you hear verbatim or occasionally paraphrase what is being said in your own words to ensure you understand what is being said.

Practice the SOFTEN method to show your engagement. The acronym stands for Smile, Open, Forward, Touch, Eye, Nod.

You can try these techniques out of the office as well or merely listen to others having conversations to hear where these techniques might help them.

Related Practices
Powerful Questions
The Silent Count

Build SMART Goals

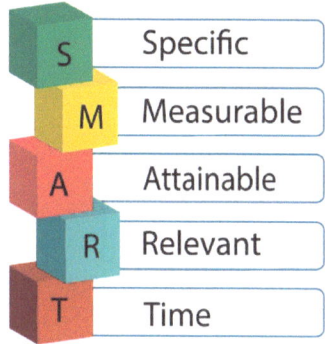

Vague, open-ended goals usually fail. Try building SMART goals.

S	Specific
M	Measurable
A	Attainable
R	Relevant
T	Time

The Practice
When defining a goal (e.g. a retrospective action), using the SMART acronym as a guideline for defining it can be very useful. The acronym stands for:

- Specific – Target a specific area for improvement.
    - Ask who, what, when, where and how. Vague goals can drag on.
- Measurable – Quantify or at least suggest an indicator of progress.
    - If you want to reduce defects or build times, provide some numbers that you can shoot for and measure.
- Attainable – What results can realistically be achieved, given who is available
    - This isn't the place for stretch goals. They have to be realistic
- Relevant - Ensure that the goal matters, that it has meaning and is worthwhile.
    - Don't create work goals. Create goals that will change how you work or change your career trajectory.
- Time - Create a deadline.
    - Open-ended or non-existent deadlines allow the matters of the day to distract us from completing other goals.

Examples
- "I will learn about test-driven development, write some example code and demonstrate it to a group at a Pizza Wednesday before the end of the month".
- "We will implement 360 Reviews, have each team complete a round and receive the results by September 1st".
- "We will impose WiP Limits on our task board during the next Sprint".

Dot Voting

A quick way to gauge consensus within a group

Ray Gun	9 Votes
Disco Rifle	5 Votes
Plasma SMG	8 Votes
Ultra Blade	8 Votes

Getting a group of people (developers, stakeholders, etc.) to converge towards an agreement can be challenging, especially on complex issues. Dot voting is a helpful practice for measuring consensus and also for making decisions.

The Practice
The steps for dot voting are:
- Write the voting choices on large sticky notes or index cards.
- Explain the choices and the steps to the group.
- If each person gets more than one vote (see tips below), explain that they can distribute the votes however they like (all votes for one choice or spread out among multiple choices).
- Using stickers or markers, have people gather around the list and place or mark their votes.
- Count the dots for each choice and mark (or move) them based on the votes they received.

Tips
- A formula for figuring out how many dot votes each person gets is the "one third plus one" rule. Take the number of choices given, divide it by three and add one. For example, if there are nine choices, each person gets four votes.
- Before voting, get the group to agree to the results if the results will be used to decide.
- Using tokens that can be moved have the benefit of allowing voters to modify their vote if they change their mind.

Fishbone a Problem

Use a graphical tree to find the root cause of a tricky problem

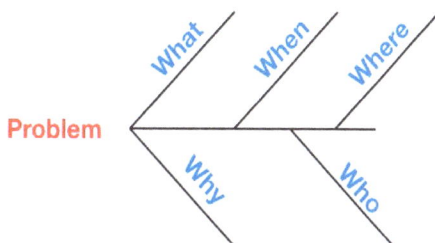

Problem

What / When / Where / Why / Who

Fishboning is another activity that teams can use for root cause analysis.

The Practice
A facilitator will draw an empty fishbone diagram on a large whiteboard and label the problem at the head of the fish, on the left. They will then identify the initial bones (contributing factors) branching out from the spine for the team to drill down into. A good generic list of bones are "What", "Why", "When", "Where and "Who". The team then branches out the bones focusing on one at a time, often using "The Five Whys" to get more detail and flesh out the skeleton looking for root causes that can then be solved.

Examples
- One team found that iteration times were too long and created a fishbone diagram with bones for slow compile times, art iteration process, QA turn-around, broken builds, discipline separation, etc. By looking at all the contributing factors and finding a number of root causes, they were able to cut their iteration times in half.
- One team fishboned the root causes of why they were so disengaged as a team in their retrospective. The root causes were related to the distribution of work where the leads and managers were doing things that the team wanted to do on their own.

Related Practices
The 5 Whys

GROW the Future

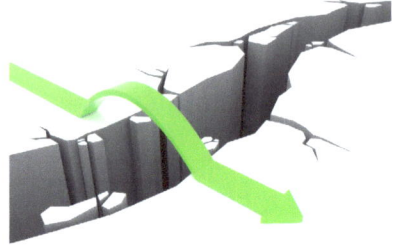

Use the GROW model to help people create solutions, navigate the future and grow their careers

Grow is a four-step model, whose acronym means:

- **G**oal
- Current **R**eality
- **O**ptions (or Obstacles)
- **W**ill (or Way Forward)

The Practice

Follow the four steps of the GROW model as follows:

1. Establish a goal that addresses the problem or behavior that needs to change. This is expressed as a SMART Goal.
2. Establish the current reality. Ask Powerful Questions to elicit exactly what is happening while practicing Active Listening.
3. Explore all the options. Identify all the obstacles to implementing the goal. This is another area where asking Powerful Questions come in handy. Questions like:
   - What needs to start happening?
   - What needs to stop happening?
   - If you were in charge, what would you do?
   - If that option didn't work, what would be your "Plan B"?
4. Establish a commitment to achieving the goal. Using the SMART Goal criteria, identify a date or timebox that the goal will be achieved. Also use binary criteria that will indicate with a 'yes or no', whether it has been achieved or not.

Related Practices

Ask Powerful Questions
Actively Listen
Build SMART Goals

Planning Poker

Discuss and measure things using this collaborative group method

Planning poker is a practice that fosters group conversation about things we need to discuss and measure such as:
- Time estimates of tasks
- Size estimates of user stories
- Risk probabilities
- Priorities
- Etc.

The Practice

A group convenes with each person holding a deck of planning poker cards with a range of numbers on them. A facilitator will go through the following steps:
1. Read an item out to the group.
2. Allow a few minutes for discussion about the item.
3. Have everyone vote simultaneously using one of their cards.
4. Discuss and resolve any outlying votes (highest and lowest numbers).
5. Re-vote until there is convergence with one number.

Tips
- Try to stay between 1 and 10 on numbers (break down larger ones)
- Use the Fibonacci scale to avoid false precision with large ranges of numbers
- If a person holding out one number different from the others and no amount of discussion can change their mind, ask them to agree with the others so the group can move along

References
Mike Cohn's useful guide for using planning poker for story point estimation. He sells great planning poker cards here as well.
CreativeAgilityTools.com/PlanningPoker

Rank Ordering

A collaborative group approach to ordering a set of items

Rank ordering is a mapping practice that allows a group of people to sort, order or prioritize a list of items (such as user stories, bugs, etc.) into a single list.

The Practice
- Items are presented on cards (one per card) and are spread out in random order in front of the group so that they can be easily read.
- The cards are then collected back into a deck.
- A card is drawn from the top and placed in the middle of a space (table or wall if you can stick them).
- Each member takes a card from the stack and places it above/below or alongside other cards based on whether that card has a higher proposed order, the same or lower than the others on the list.
- Instead of placing a card, a member can swap two existing cards on the table if they disagree with how they are placed. This continues until the deck is emptied.

Tips
- If two cards are swapped often, a facilitator should ask questions to determine the best order.
- Rank ordering can be used to sort user story sizes. The ranked list can then be divided into story point buckets or t-shirt sizes.

Related Practices
T-shirt sizing

Roman Voting

A quick way to measure a group's opinion

Legend holds that in Roman times, a defeated gladiator's fate was decided by the emperor. If he gave a thumbs up sign, the gladiator was allowed to live and a thumbs down sign indicated he could be finished off by the victor. This practice is much less radical, but is very useful.

The Practice
When we want to measure a group's opinion or decision on a particular question, a roman vote can take seconds to give us the result. The practice is simple. The group is asked a question and they simultaneously give their response with either a thumbs up (a yes vote) or a thumbs down (a no vote).

Tips
- Remind everyone to vote simultaneously and discourage those who wait to observe the group's vote before they vote themselves.
- The thumb-sideways vote option can be added to indicate that one is "undecided".
- If the majority is not clear, you can have everyone hold their vote up while you count each thumbs up and thumbs down vote.

Start Meetings Efficiently

Eliminate the 5 to 10 minutes wasted at the start of meetings

This is a collection of tips you can use to get your meetings off to an efficient and effective start.

The Practice
- Have someone 'own' the meeting (the meeting owner).
- The meeting owner arrives 5-10 minutes early (so no back-to-back meetings).
- The meeting owner sets up the room and makes sure all the equipment works (projection, video conferencing system, etc.).

Tips
- Know when to timebox and when to end early. If there is an agenda for the meeting, end the meeting as soon as the agenda is complete. If the meeting is timeboxed, the meeting owner should enforce it diligently.
- As a variation, use 'The Thinking Environment Meeting' in which you have an open round question of the day which is related to the problem that is being solved. Allow each person to talk about it for 2 minutes without interruption.

Table Challenge

Generate fresh insights on a problem through challenges

Often, having a fresh set of eyes can help to solve problems and come up with new ideas. Inviting another group to join in for this purpose is a great way to move through challenges.

The Practice
An even number of groups of people (team, discipline group, etc.) sit at tables and write down any ideas that need to be thought through, as well as any challenges that need to be addressed on cards (one per card).

When the groups are ready they exchange cards and add their recommendations on the cards. They then take turns reading out what is written on the cards and after a card each card is addressed, a new card is written up with an agreed upon solution or improved idea.

Tips
- The groups don't have to be the same size, but there needs to be an even number of tables.
- You can add a scoring system where tables get a point when they solve a problem.

World Café

A World Café is a practice that facilitates the sharing of knowledge through relaxed, group conversation

The Practice
- A facilitator sets up a space with tables and materials where small groups of people can meet to address questions. The questions can either be identified ahead of time or by the entire group at the start. There is one question per table.
- The facilitator welcomes the group and explains the practice to them.
- The group divides up across the tables and begins a 20 minute discussion about each question at each table.
- After 20 minutes, all the groups rotate to another table. Before rotating, each table decides whether to have a "table host" remain behind to explain the discussion in the previous cycle.
- The group goes through 3 or 4 cycles and then the results of all discussions are shared with the entire group.

Tips
- Equip each table with a flip chart, easel and markers to graphically record key points.
- Find topic champions to follow up on any action items that are decided upon.

Related Practices
Open Space

References
CreativeAgilityTools.com/WorldCafe

Section 4 - Individual Growth

Buddy System

Have someone help onboard a new team member

New members can be reluctant to ask for help from teammates who are busy. Having someone who allocates a portion of their time to help onboard a new member can remedy this situation.

The Practice
When someone new joins a team, a member of the team volunteers a part of their available time to be their "buddy". Their highest priority will be to help and mentor the team member by walking them through the main practices of the team and pairing up with them during their initial work.

Tips
- Initially allocate 50% of your time to the new member and then adjust it at the next iteration (over allocating is better than under-allocating).
- Include the new member in the team's social activities like lunch and other social gatherings.
- Avoid having the new member take on any urgent or critical work.

Cross-Interview

Stimulate knowledge sharing and problem solving

The cross-interview allows team members to interview one another on questions they are familiar with in order to hear different perspectives and drive knowledge sharing.

The Practice

Team members prepare lists of questions on topics they are familiar with and interview other team members about those questions. Then they swap roles where the interviewer becomes the interviewee.

Tips

- Ask questions that are within the discipline/domain of the interviewee.
- A variation could include making it like the Jeopardy(™) game show.
- Focus on knowledge sharing and make sure the interviewee has learned something.

Example questions

- What is the best mechanical interface to use for a user control?
- What's the easiest way for a device to detect that a particular user is in view?
- How can we display a device state in the simplest possible way?

Individual Health

Check on the health and effectiveness of your team

It's good to know exactly what people on your team are thinking about your project. It is especially important to know how they feel about the leadership and the team and any blockers they might be facing. One on ones with direct managers is an effective way to get this information but it is also a good idea to meet on a quarterly basis with their Scrum Master to talk about the process, the team, and any blockers they may be facing.

The Practice
Once a quarter have an informal one on one meeting with each person on the team, and ask them questions about topics you would like to discuss with them. Some examples of topics you can discuss are: morale, blockers, team health, things they enjoy, project leadership etc. Ask them how they would go about making improvements on each item. Once you have interviewed everyone, put together a list of items to review with members of the leadership team to find optimal ways to deal with any issues that come up, as well as ways to celebrate successes.

Tips
- This is a great way to identify and quickly remove blockers as sometimes people don't think their "little blocker" is affecting anyone else.
- You can also do this frequently using a roman vote to gauge if people are feeling engaged (thumbs up) or disengaged (thumbs down). Remember to have everyone vote simultaneously.

Initiation Project

Create a project that a new employee can implement to best learn the ropes

When people join a company, they are often thrown into the work expecting to understand how to navigate the "ins and outs" of your process, technology and build systems. This can create the potential for fear and costly failure. An initiation project is a good way for them to solve a known problem while learning about and implementing the process and using the tools in a safe and educational manner.

The Practice
Create a project for the new team member to work on in a time-box. The project should have been previously solved for a benchmark and have a set of user stories describing the desired outcome.

The goals of the project are for the new team member to:
- Communicate requirements with a customer or product owner
- Learn who to ask for help
- Identify gaps in the documentation for existing systems
- Have a broad exposure to the main areas of technology and the systems that are required for building and deployment

Tips
- Ask someone to be the Product Owner.
- Ask someone else to be the Scrum Master or coach who can help them overcome problems.
- Have a retrospective after the time-box to discuss the results.
- Regardless of the results have a ceremony to celebrate their "initiation" to the team and give them a "Viking Point."

Related Practices
Time Boxing
Viking Points

LEGO™ Tracking

Visually track how much time is spent on unplanned work

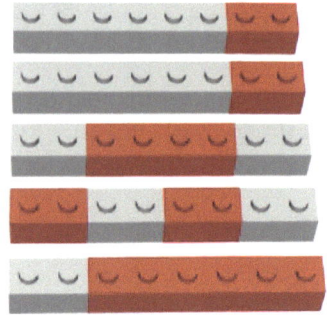

The Practice

Each developer has a few red and white LEGO bricks that represent a chunk of time. Throughout each day, they snap a brick onto a plate based on whether the time they've spent since the last brick snapped was on planned work or unplanned work. Over the course of the day, week or iteration, they build up a visual 3D image of how much time is spent on planned vs unplanned work.

Tips

- You can add categories, such as bug fixing and meetings using different colored bricks.
- A simple timer (such as on an app on a smartphone) can be used if a reminder is needed when it is time to add a new brick.
- The plates or simply a count of the red bricks can be brought to the retrospective.
- The goal isn't to eliminate unplanned work, but to be aware of where it is coming from and manage it if it is growing too large.

Struggle Ducky

Build your team culture and help
anyone who has a rubber duck

The Practice
Each team has a single rubber duck,
called a "Struggle Ducky" which is used
for rubber duck debugging. Anyone on
the team who is struggling with an issue grabs the duck and talks to it
in the hope of figuring out a solution. If the conversation continues long
enough, the rest of the team can come to the aid of the team member
(and duck).

Team leaders can also identify those who are having prolonged or
multiple issues, by looking at who has been speaking with Struggle
Ducky the most.

Tips
- If one seeks the Struggle Ducky and finds that another team
  member is already in conversation, they should join that
  conversation to help the first team member. When their
  problem is solved, all three can focus on the second issue.
- The duck should be returned to its proper place when the
  issue has been resolved.

Section 5 - Iteration Improvements

Art Verification Column

Not Started	Work in Progress	Verification Needed (3)	Done
Asset	Asset	Asset	Asset
Asset		Asset	Asset
		Asset	

Add a column to a task board that holds assets waiting for approval

A common problem is having a large number of assets being rejected by an art director or lead at the end of a sprint. Adding a verification column to hold those assets that are considered done by an artist creates an opportunity for feedback in the sprint. This can reduce the amount of effort that is wasted and can create opportunities for mentoring.

The Practice
Add a column to a sprint task board before the "done" column. Any asset that is visible in the product and is considered to be done has its task card placed in that column until it has received approval from an art lead. At the end of the sprint, that column, along with the WiP column, must be empty.

Tips
- Put a WiP limit on the verification column. When that limit is reached, the Scrum Master is allowed to drag the art lead over by the ear and review the assets waiting.
- Try to review the asset in the product. Reviewing it in an art tool can lead to rejection when it's seen in the product later.

Related Practices
- Use WiP Limits

Bug Bash

Determine which bugs need to be fixed to ship

The goal of every product is to ship bug free, but we all know that is impossible. One way to help the team march to completion is to have a daily bug bash meeting to determine which bugs get priority.

The Practice
- This practice is used at the stage when you are only fixing bugs, and hopefully not adding more features.
- Have a daily meeting with all leads & POs where you can review new bugs that have come in and determine how to deal with them.
- Bugs should have a priority set and you should decide if they need to be fixed this iteration before release.
- Every few days you need to review all of the bugs in your active database and determine what must still be fixed.
- Every few days eliminate another priority level:
  - Example: On day one of bug bash stop, fixing priority 4s.
  - By the end of the bug bash you should only be fixing priority 0 and 1s.
- Make sure the team is aware of what bugs you are still fixing. (For example, 0s, 1s & 2s)

Tips
- Make sure everyone in the room gets to speak up on each bug.
- Not everyone has the same priorities coming into the room, so make sure to establish the priorities right away in each meeting:
- "We are only focused on totally blocking issues, cosmetic issues will have to wait."
- Make sure QA has someone present and they are aware of each decision. This can help them focus on what types of bugs to keep chasing down.

Burndown Your PBIs

Measure your daily progress adding features into the product

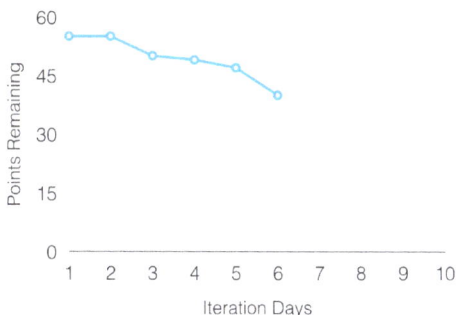

The Problem
An iteration burndown chart typically shows the hours remaining for unfinished tasks, but a smooth burndown of hours can hide unfinished work that is piling up. Features left undone until the end of the iteration eliminate opportunities to iterate and improve them. Additional work often emerges during the final effort to integrate features and can lead to an end-of-iteration crunch that compromises quality.

Visualizing PBIs as completed puts the emphasis on completing features instead of completing tasks.

The Practice
The practice is to burndown the product backlog items (PBIs) or stories *only when they are done*. This requires that either the PBI sizes are measured (in story points, etc.) and/or are broken down into smaller, similarly-sized items (e. g. t-shirt sized).

After iteration planning, add up the numbers or sizes of PBIs. This number is your starting burndown size on day 1. Every time a PBI is completed (meets the definition of done), its size is subtracted from the remaining total on the burndown chart.

Tips
- Expect the burndown to be flat at the start of the iteration. If no PBIs are completed during the first week, ask the team about it. The PBIs may need to be broken down further or the team may need to prioritize their work differently.
- An iteration backlog estimate burndown (hours or days) can still be used but the PBI burndown should be the primary, visible chart.

Related Practices
Talk to the board
T-shirt sizing

Estimate in Days, not Hours

If hour estimates are too precise, don't use them

Instead of estimating iteration backlog tasks in hours, try estimating them in days. When teams work on new, uncertain features and then estimate the work in hours, the result can be highly precise estimates that are not very accurate. This wastes time in iteration planning and does not benefit the team's ability to forecast and track their iteration.

Estimating in days can take less time and be just as accurate (if not more) than estimating in hours.

The Practice
At the start of iteration planning, hand out one index card for every working day of the iteration to each team member (I. e. if you have a two-week iteration with a day of review, retrospective and planning, hand out nine cards to each team member).

During iteration planning, team members capture iteration backlog tasks on the index cards. If they can get two tasks done in a day, they write them down on one card. If a task takes a couple of days, then they staple two cards together and write the task down on the top.

During the daily standup, cards are simply moved between "not-started", "in-progress" and "done" columns.

Tips
- Updating the iteration backlog is quick. So is the iteration burndown - you just count cards outside the done column.
- Added practices, like adding a daily hash-mark on every card in the "in progress" column can highlight tasks that are stalled.
- If you put multiple tasks on a single card, you can chop up the card or just mark off each task on the card and only move it once all sub-day tasks have been completed. Allow the team to decide on they want to do this.

Feature Flow Cards

Manage workflow on a cross-discipline feature that requires some hand-offs

Killer Robots

As a player, my character encounters industrial robot arms which attack me as I pass them

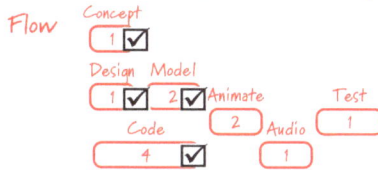

Flow

Concept
1 ☑

Design   Model
1 ☑   2 ☑ Animate   Test
            Code   2) Audio   1)
            4   ☑   (1)

The Practice

The Feature flow card starts life as a user story (PBI): "As a user, I want the device to wake up when I enter the room and display an animation of its state". During iteration planning, the team identifies and draws a simple flowchart of the work required and dependencies/hand-offs for the feature. Work that is dependent on previous work is drawn to the right of the dependency. In the example card above, there is some design and concept work that modeling is dependent on, however coding of the behavior can begin right away.

The flowchart is pretty simple. Each box represents specialization work as well as the number of days they expect to take before being able to hand off the work to the next specialist. For example, a couple of days of modeling may be needed before animation can begin. Boxes can overlap when there isn't a dependency.

Unlike a Gantt chart, this isn't a schedule but just a forecast of the work. Since the team is working on multiple stories, this flow may take up to two weeks to accomplish.

As the team works through the iteration, they discuss their progress through the flow and check off specialist dependencies on the card as they are handed off.

Tips

- While planning, use a whiteboard or sticky notes to model the flow.
- Teams can even leave out the estimates in the boxes if that works better for them.
- Try to avoid using individual names if more than one person can work on a task.

Fix-it Friday

Manage debt by setting aside every Friday to fix, polish and fine tune the product

The Practice
Every Friday unallocated time is used to bring the entire product to a "definition of done" for the iteration.

Tips
- Account for 4-day weeks when planning your iteration.
- Don't let Fix-it Friday be a dumping ground for sloppy work done during the week. All blocking of bugs should be fixed as soon as they occur.
- Use Fix-it Friday for other, unscheduled things such as HR meetings, etc. This allows the rest of the week to be focused on the iteration.
- If you have iteration reviews on Fridays, account for this in your planning as you can't have both review and Fix-it Friday on the same day.
- Fix-it Friday can start with a quick triage in the morning about the goal for the day.

Iteration Reviews

Celebrate the amazing accomplishments of the team

At the end of each iteration, it's a good idea to celebrate the success of the project by allowing each team the opportunity to show off what they have accomplished. The most effective way to do this is to replace your weekly team meeting with an iteration review, also called "a dog and pony show".

The Practice

At the end of each iteration have every team put together a brief presentation (of under 5 minutes) on what they have accomplished this iteration. Encourage them to show videos over slideshows. Each iteration randomize the order of the teams and make sure that every team does a presentation even if it's just one member getting up and saying a few words. Keep the meeting short *and don't leave time for Q & A*. When a team is finished move on to the next team, when everyone has gone the meeting is over. This encourages people with questions to go to the team directly.

Tips

- Make sure that people aren't spending hours on a presentation.
- Have some sort of snack for everyone.
- Keep it light hearted and exciting, cheer loudly for successes.
- Make sure the whole project is involved, especially QA.

Related Practices

Sprint Day

Multi-Team Sprint Goal Refinement

For teams working in areas that are coupled and have potential dependencies, syncing on design and preliminary sprint planning reduces dependencies

If for example you have three teams that are working on user interface design, the chance of dependencies between these teams that will impede their chances of achieving sprint goals will be higher.

A useful practice is to have all three teams (or at least representatives from each team) meet to discuss design and refine sprint goals before each team plans their sprints separately.

The Practice
Before every sprint, have multi-team meetings for team members (or representatives from each team) to meet and discuss the upcoming goal for their feature area so they can:
- Make agreements over sharing a specialist's time in areas where the teams might be experiencing conflicts
- Remove any duplication of effort by deciding which team might take on the effort and prioritize the work appropriately so the other team(s) don't get blocked
- Explore areas of collaboration so a small cross-team unit can be formed to solve a shared problem and provide solutions for each team as part of the upcoming sprint commitment

Tips
- Time-box these meetings to 30 minutes
- Capture agreements that can be taken into the teams' sprint planning sessions to ensure they are followed through on
- Hold regular mini Scrum-of-Scrum meetings to address progress

Related practices
If this is connected to any other practice, you can mention this practice

Reference
http://less.works (cross-team meetings)

Priority Status Board

Create transparency
for iteration priorities

The Practice
Display the priorities from iteration planning and execution on a visible board.
Place a colored sticky note to indicate the status beside each of the priorities.

Example color codes:
- Yellow: "Not started yet"
- Green: "Done!"
- Blue: "Not done, but in progress without any blockers"
- Pink: "Complicated and uncertain"
- Red: "Struggling. There are blockers"

Tips
- Change status of priorities in a transparent way (e. g. in the daily stand-up)
- Once the sticky-notes are placed next to each category, create a list beside the priority board with action items for the day for each priority category that doesn't have a green sticky.

Related Practices
War room

Sprint Day

	Mon	Tue	Wed	Thu	Fri
	1	2	3	4	5
	6	7	8	9	10 Sprint Day

"Sprint Day"

- Sprint Review
- Lunch
- Retrospective
- Sprint Planning

Review, retrospect and plan the next sprint in a day!

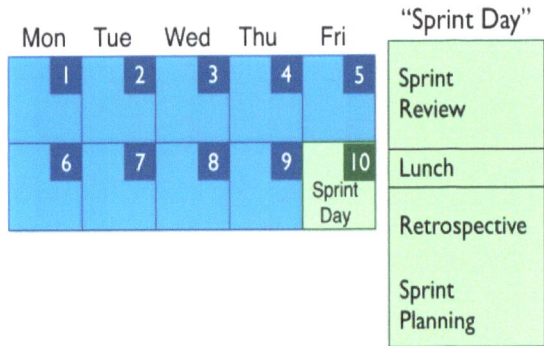

The Practice

Some teams spend a couple of days every sprint reviewing, retrospecting and planning. For a two-week sprint, that represents 20% of the available time! While that time might be required when teams are first forming, or while there is a lot of exploration going on during the product, optimizing the schedule will allow you more time for development.

An example of this is called the "Sprint Day". This is when teams will hold a review and retrospect about the completed sprint during the first half of the day and then plan the next sprint during the second half of the day.

The calendar above shows the sprint day occurring every other Friday for a two-week sprint, but in practice a sprint day can also work for three-week sprints. The image to the right shows a rough breakdown of the day:

- The sprint review is held in the morning.
- Retrospectives are held right after lunch (or just before, if the teams finish early enough).
- The remainder of the day is allocated to planning for the next sprint.

Tips

- Holding the sprint day on Fridays works well as the team will enjoy the weekend off more knowing their plan and they can hit-the-ground running on Monday.
- If you have a large product with multiple teams, it's best to have a single review with an integrated build, followed by separate team retrospectives and planning sessions.
- For this to work well, it is best to have a well-refined product backlog. Holding a backlog refinement meeting 2-3 days before the end of the sprint will help you to achieve this.

Swim Lanes

Create, visualize and track a work category for solving urgent requests

Ready (5)	Design (3)	Develop (5)	Buffer	Test (4)	Done
		Feature	Feature	Feature	Feature
		Feature		Feature	
Feature	Feature	Feature			
Urgent Request				Urgent Request	
		Urgent Request			Urgent Request

Scrum teams which support live product or work they've previously deployed are challenged with how to account and manage such support work within an iteration. How do they commit to an iteration goal when they'll get unavoidable interruptions to solve problems? One practice is to carve out a **swim lane** on their task board to track the support work.

The Practice
A swim lane is a row on a task board that contains a separate class of work (see illustration above). By creating this separate class, we can apply different behaviors (policies) for how we treat this work. For example, support work often needs to be worked on quickly by an expert on the team. Rather than mixing up urgent work on the task board, a separate lane makes it more visible.

Example usage
- One team supporting a product used red cards that signaled that a support request had the highest urgency (e.g. An exploit was found). When a red card was in a column (such as for a test), it forced all other testing in that column to come to a halt to support that work.
- One team of eight developers set aside 50% of their time for support work (based on the tracking emergent work practice). Each day, during the daily stand-up, they decided which four developers would be working on tasks in the support swim lane.
- Since swim lane work is emergent, the product owner can prioritize the order in which support work is pulled into the lane. This prevents people from various groups bombarding the developers with prioritization requests.

Related Practices
Track Emergent Work

The "Done Done" Column

Not Started	Work in Progress	Done	Done Done
Task	Task	Task	Task
Task		Task	Task
		Task	

Elevate the role of quality in your iterations

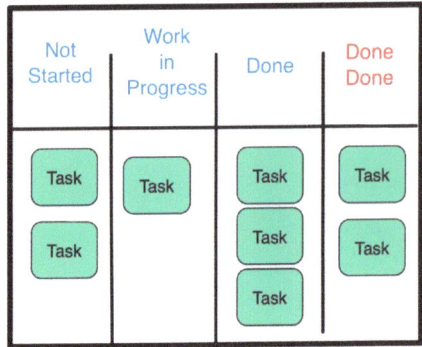

While quality assurance is every developer's responsibility, the depth, complexity and interconnectedness of software means that they benefit greatly from someone using the software for the purpose of testing it at every stage of development. Companies often struggle with whether this responsibility should be given to one individual who is dedicated to the role, or if it is better as a shared responsibility. Either way, one thing is certain - it should be part of an iteration.

The Practice
The "done done" column is a column added to the right side of a task board, beside the "done" column. When a PBI meets the "definition of done", it is placed into that column and it creates a more concrete, visible declaration that this part of the iteration goal is complete.

Tips
Integrating testers by having them join in about 20-40% of the time will help them feel more part of the team. Let them take the role of gate-keepers and decide whether PBIs are ready to be moved into the "done done" column. They can also run a test (that is often avoided by developers) which includes the feature "running on all platforms and build configurations" as part of the "definition of done".

If you are not integrating testers, have members of the team (ideally developers who were least involved in the development of a PBI) rotate the responsibility of approving the movement of PBIs to the "done done" column.

Related Practices
Burndown your PBIs

The Build Health Radiator

A simple physical device that radiates the state of the current build and raises an alarm when the build is broken for too long

A practice made famous in Toyota factories called "stop the line" was initially considered to be outrageous by Western car manufacturer's standards, but is now widely used since it leads quick problem solving and higher quality cars. In this practice, whenever any assembly line worker sees a problem, they pull a cord which alters the "problem solver". If this problem solver can't fix the problem in 20 minutes, the entire assembly line comes to a halt until it is solved.

We apply the same principle with the **Build Health Radiator**.

The Practice
The build health radiator is a device which shows the state of the latest build. It's called a radiator because it is large and visible and "radiates" information to everyone that cannot be ignored. The radiator can take many forms. Teams have used large toy traffic lights and PC tools that create pop-up dialogs on every developer's PC. A favorite is the lava lamp. When the build breaks, the lava lamp is turned on. It takes about 20 minutes for the wax inside to heat up enough for a blob to float to the top. When it reaches the top it creates a public signal to stop work. The stability team or the developer who broke the build then fixes it.

Tips
- Build tools, such as Cruise Control, have interfaces that allow developers to integrate this behavior into the desktops of all the developers.
- There is usually someone on the team who likes to build devices using Arduino technology. Challenge them to build a radiator for your team

Related Practices
For a stability team
The blessed build indicator
Lighten the mood

The Build Monkey

Use a clean PC to firewall changes before you release it to others

Is it safe to grab the latest code changes? Are the changes I'm about to commit going to break the build? The larger the group working on the product, the more urgent these questions become. A practice that ensures the code and asset changes are safe to commit globally using a **build monkey**.

The Practice
A build monkey is a PC that has all the development tools needed to grab the latest code and assets and to build and run the product. The difference between a build monkey and a developer's PC is that no work is done on it. It is a "clean" machine used to merge changes and to build and test the product.

There are many variations on how the build monkey is used. The basic practice is that whenever someone commits a change (and they have merged all the recent changes and tested them on own their machine), they initiate a merge and build and test it on the build monkey to confirm that their changes will not break the build for everyone else.

When this practice is ignored and a commit is made that breaks the build for the entire group, there is usually a punishment for the offending individual. (Like the Justin Bieber example mentioned earlier).

Tips
- This practice can become easier by automating the build monkey process
- Improvements also include having a target platform attached to the build monkey to run tests.
- Have one build monkey per team and a "holding branch" to hold changes to be merged into the main branch once the changes have passed the build monkey tests.

Related Practices
Lighten the Mood

Track Emergent Work

Don't just track the work
you predicted, but also what you didn't

Iteration planning is based on the goal and the capacity of the team.
Capacity is empirical, which means that it is based on the amount of
work the team was able to complete, on average, in past iterations.
That work can be divided into two types:
1. Planned work
2. Unplanned work

The second type is just as important and should be accounted for
because it impacts iteration forecasting just as much as the first.

The Practice
During the iteration, new work will emerge. This work usually falls into
a few categories:
A. Bugs
B. Extra tuning time
C. Work we didn't (or couldn't) foresee in the planning stage

Rather than just adding more time to an existing task, try creating a
new task to tackle this work. At the end of the iteration, total up all that
new work. Track this emergent work over time, based on its category
and use it in retrospectives to find ways to reduce it. Ask the following
questions for each of these categories:
A. (Bugs) - How can we improve testing and development practices?
B. (Tuning) - Are there better tools we can create to tune faster?
C. (Unplanned) - How can we plan better?

Tips
- Create a burndown chart of emergent work per iteration and
  post it on the team wall.
- Plot a burn-up line of emergent work as a new line on the
  burndown chart.
- Expect emergent work to increase based on the amount of
  uncertainty involved - Don't react negatively to it.
- If you use a task-board, use different colored cards or sticky
  notes for emergent types of work.

Use WiP Limits

Limit the amount of work-in-progress so teams can focus on getting things done

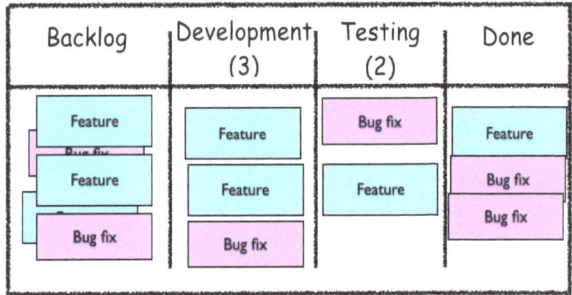

Backlog	Development (3)	Testing (2)	Done
Feature	Feature	Bug fix	Feature
Feature	Feature	Feature	Bug fix
Bug fix	Bug fix		Bug fix

If a lot of work-in-progress (WiP) piles up, nothing will get done until the end of the iteration. The problem with this is that finishing the work often takes more time than we anticipate and can lead to the late iteration crunch which often compromises quality. A WiP limit can help prevent this.

The Practice
WiP limits require placing a restriction on the number of items that can be in-progress at any one time. It is represented by a number at the top of the in-progress column (determined by the team at the start of the iteration) of a task board (WiP limits are often supported by electronic tools).

The basic rule is that when the number of tasks in the in-progress column reaches the WiP limit, no further tasks can be pulled into that column from the not started column until a task is completed. This creates challenges for teams that have a lot of impediments or slow processes (like long approval cycles) and puts pressure on them to come up with solutions.

Tips
- Challenge the team to reduce the WiP limits a little bit each iteration. This will continually identify the next process impediments.
- You can also place WiP limits on other columns, such as testing.
- If you have a separate testing column, you can add a column between in progress and testing for tasks or features that are ready for testing. This buffer column can also have a WiP limit and when it is reached, a few hours of assistance may be required from the development team.

The War Room

Set aside a space where teams can host their iteration artifacts and daily standup meetings

If you have the luxury of unused rooms or offices, converting one to a war room has some benefits for teams over an open space or hallway.

The Practice
Commandeer a room with as much wall space as possible and mount the team's iteration task board and any other artifacts the team will use on a day-to-day basis (such as the love wall, open topic board, etc.). Teams will also hold their daily standups in this room.

Tips
- Based on available wall space, multiple teams can share the same room. One 10 foot by 10 foot room hosted three teams. The teams negotiate their daily standup schedule to avoid overlap.
- Ban chairs, tables and any other furniture from this room.

WiP Tokens

A simple visual way to protect specialists from being overwhelmed

Software development has a large number of specialized roles that makes creating cross-disciplinary teams of full-time members nearly impossible. For example, many teams find that they need only part of a UX designer's time, so a designer might split work across two or three teams during an iteration. Since this is based on the timing of each team's needs, they will likely have too little or too much work to do. Multitasking on more than three things results in a loss of productivity.

Work-in-Progress (WiP) tokens are designed to prevent team members from exceeding this limit.

The Practice
This practice requires that you bring three tokens (that will stick to your task boards) with you when attending daily stand-up meetings. Once you announce that you'll start working on a PBI, you attach your token to the PBI (or the associated task you are working on) on the board. *This token will only be removed when your work is done.* This process is continued until you run out of free (unattached) tokens. Then when you are asked to work on something, you can point out that you have a full workload and can't take on more work.

Tips
- Make sure the teams you work with are aware of your policy before the iteration starts. Don't just unilaterally decide to do it.
- If teams use a whiteboard that magnets stick to, then you can use three magnets of the same color. Otherwise, you can use sticky tokens or pieces of paper you can pin on a cork board.
- If a specialist is subject to urgent requests that can't be ignored, they can reserve a token for emergencies.

Section 6 - Project Management

Buy a Feature

Decide which features to "buy" first when you have a limited budget or limited time.

When a group of people have a list of things they want to buy (build, purchase, etc.) and not enough budget (time, cost, etc.) to buy them all, 'Buy a feature' is an effective collaboration game to play.

The Practice
The main stakeholders who have a list of features gather together.

- The features are written down on index cards (one per feature) along with a cost for each (cash, points, etc.).
- A set of tokens that represent the budget available in the currency of the features is distributed among the stakeholders.
- All stakeholders are asked to distribute their tokens across the features as they see fit.
- A discussion is held about the set of features that are either fully or partially purchased.
- Step 3 and 4 are repeated until the set of features purchased closely matches the budget.

Tips
- The overall game and steps 3 and 4 should be time-boxed.
- The person who facilitates this game should not be a stakeholder.
- Monopoly money works well as a currency token.
- Try to limit the group to 5-9 stakeholders.
- It's useful to "mark the money" so you can keep track who is spending the money and where it is being spent as you repeat steps 3 and 4.
- It's best to distribute the currency equally, but there may be times when some stakeholders will be required to receive more than others.

Define Product Pillars

Define your product's pillars
to help drive cohesive
decision making

One of the quickest and simplest ways to gain alignment on a product is to define it clearly and explicitly; what it is and what it isn't etc. One simple way to do that is by creating Product Pillars. These are clearly defined words that the product and its features are measured against. Here are examples of Pillars from video game Diablo 3: approachable, powerful heroes, highly customizable, great item game, endlessly replayable, strong setting, and cooperative multiplayer.

The Practice
- Sit down with your leadership team and discuss what the core parts of your product are.
- While you are discussing these aspects have one person write them on a board.
- Once you have gone through all of the features, group them together.
- Now come up with pillars for each group.
- If you have too many pillars do a MoSCoW pass on the items.
- Once you have defined your pillars, inform the team in a meeting and place the pillars somewhere they are highly visible.

Tips
- Consider making a Propaganda Poster using the Pillars
- Whenever new features are requested, ask this question: "Does that fit the pillars?"
- You can use the 'Back of the Box' to help inform everyone of your pillars

Related Practices
MoSCoW
Propaganda Posters
Back of The Box

Embrace Risk

A technique for managing risk throughout a project

Technology development has a host of risks, from the market's whims changing rapidly, to new hardware appearing. It is an ever-changing landscape. As a result, many products fail to achieve their goals or developers are asked to work miracles. Many of these problems could be avoided if people embraced risk instead of avoiding it and accepted that inevitably things go wrong from time to time.

The Practice
- Create a list of possible risks (use an ideation practice such as a Premortem) with all developers.
- Prioritize the risks according to impact and probability (see the Risk Prioritization Matrix practice).

Take the most impactful and likely risks and identify the following:
- The trigger date or condition (also called risk transition).
- Example: if this critical middleware isn't ported to this hardware platform by October
- Mitigation strategy (including a plan and cost for eliminating the risk)
- Example: Six engineers working for two months to port the middleware ourselves
- Communicate this risk strategy plan widely with all of the stakeholders.
- Revisit the plan on a regular basis (once every iteration)

Tips
- Create and distribute a risk strategy plan. Additionally, follow-up with key stakeholders to ensure that they have signed off on the plan.

Related Practices
Premortems
Risk Prioritization Matrix

References
Book: Waltzing with Bears - Tom DeMarco

Form a Stability Team

Create a team that refines the craft of higher quality

A major agile value is to build product quality (stability, efficiency, fun and polish) along the way, rather than building quality into the product at the end of a project. Implementing this value can be a challenge since there is often a strong temptation to add untested prototype features into a product at a rapid rate and worry about making them run well later.

Although the goal is to grow a culture that supports building quality increments with every team, an effective tool to use in the interim is to create a **stability team** whose focus is to help other teams grow their focus on quality.

The Practice

The stability team is a support team which may assist with a backlog of work building tools, improving the content pipeline, adding shared technology, etc. But they also have another mandate, which is to grow the stability of the build throughout development by finding the root cause of problems and either solving them or coaching teams on how to improve their practices. For example, our stability team found out that poorly named skeleton joints were causing about 10% of the crashes in the product. By improving an exporter to filter such names, they improved the stability of the build for everyone.

Tips

- Have the product send an email every time it crashed to an email alias indicating who was using the product, stack information and other useful data. This helps the stability team track down the root cause.
- Another useful tool was a chart which showed the overall stability of the product throughout the day using the automated tests. It was a big motivational tool for the team to see stability rise from 30% to 95% over six months.

Related Practices

The Blessed Build Indicator
Use Swim Lanes

Product Box

Establish a shared vision of a product or feature among the team

Creating a shared vision among the team can be a challenge. Not everyone reads the big design document and those who do can still have different views of the product. Cross-discipline conversation is the best and quickest way to establish a shared vision and the product box is an effective practice to use for this purpose.

The Practice
The development group gathers and each team (of 5-9 people) is given a large flip chart sheet or box and markers. They spend 20-30 minutes working with the product owner to create a mock-up box that their product or feature could theoretically be shipped in (even if it is only downloaded). Using sketch art and marketing blurbs, they illustrate the box as attractively as possible so that potential buyers will select their product from a crowded shelf of competing products. Once the boxes have been designed, each team elects a representative to present their box to the rest of the group.

Tips
- This is a useful practice to implement at the start of every release cycle (2-3 months).
- During the presentations, the product owner can speak up to clarify or correct a divergence of vision. For example, if a team's box lists "free cloud storage" as a feature and that epic is not in the product backlog, the product owner can address the reasons for its exclusion.
- Whether or not the product ships in a box, give the team the option to create a web page instead.

Kanban Cards

Track the timeline for developing features or assets from start to finish

Prop:	Crane	
Start:	2/10	
Concept:	2/12	Cycle
Model:	2/14	Time
Texture:	2/15	10 days
Approval:	2/18	
In game:	2/20	

A benefit of lean production methods is that they focus on optimizing the whole workflow, rather than the individual parts. Kanban cards are a tool that make the flow visual and allow it to be tracked, making it easier to measure it and find ways of improving it.

The Practice
Start by visualizing the workflow to capture every step that a feature or asset goes through. Create Kanban cards which have a space for recording the date when each of these steps are completed. When the feature is brought into the first stage of development (e.g. concept), record the start date.

When the feature or asset is completed and is in the product, derive the cycle time (in-product date minus start date) and write it on the card. Over time, compare the cycle time for features and assets of the same types to determine if practice experiments are improving the cycle time.

Tips
- Use a Kanban board to track the state of multiple assets and features in the pipeline.

Related Practices
Kanban board

Kano your Backlog

Balance exciting new features with the boring but necessary ones

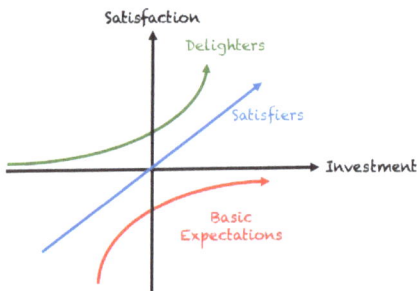

The Practice
Invite your stakeholders, product owner(s), leads and developers (if there is room) into a meeting where the major features on the product backlog will be roughly prioritized into three categories:

- **Delighters** - These are features which are rare in similar products or have never been seen before. These features are highlighted by marketing and will delight the users.
- **Satisfiers** - These are features which users are not surprised by but enjoy. Competitors may or may not have all of these.
- **Basic expectations** - These features are not advertised but are expected by the user and their absence will upset them.

Tips
- Delighters are usually the most expensive and/or riskiest features. Don't commit to too many!
- Explore ways to fulfil Satisfiers better than competitor products.
- Focus test groups are a good source of feedback for Satisfiers and Basic expectations, but not for Delighters.

Related Practices
MoSCoW analysis

LeSS™ Roles

Roles that help you scale effectively for larger products

Large-Scale Scrum (LeSS™) is a framework for scaling Scrum. For large products, it recommends the addition of certain roles to overcome some of the problems that large groups of people working together encounter. These roles are **Travelers**, **Scouts** and **Component Mentors**.

The Roles

- **Travelers** are team members on one or two teams that only stay for an iteration or two to provide assistance and to teach developers. An example is the backend expert who works with a team to set up a backend and also pairs with another programmer to write the code. Once the cloth is working the traveler leaves and the programmer remains to support the cloth effect.
- **Scouts** attend as many of the daily standups as possible and provide a progress report to the chief product owner. They also take part in release planning and backlog refinement meetings helping large teams to be more synchronized.
- **Component Mentors** are members of a feature team who reserve spare time to mentor other teams on their component (e. g. social integration) or discipline (e. g. design, programming, etc). They teach techniques and help advise teams on the best way to implement features related to their component or area of expertise.

References
less.works

Map Your Stories

Capture and visualize a narrative of features

A product's core mechanics can often be described as a narrative of features.

As a fugitive I want to race a car	Though the busy streets of Chicago	While police chase me	and I avoid obstacles
I want to drive a car	Through a grid of streets	While sirens play and lights flash if I drive slow	and some ambient traffic exists (spike)
The car has a handbrake, so I can drift	One block looks like Chicago	Police cars attempt to ram my car	Ambient moving traffic and other obstacles
I want to drive a classic Mustang	Complete Chicago	Police can stop and arrest me	

For example, "As a user, I navigate a series of menus and pages to solve my problem". This narrative implies a sequence of features that cannot be developed in isolation, but as an expanding chronicle that is poorly represented by a linear list of PBIs.

The Practice

A story map is a two-dimensional map of PBIs. The horizontal axis is a prioritized narrative of epic features and the vertical is the breakdown of each epic into smaller PBIs. The rows can be roughly mapped into iterations to produce a release plan. As the release plan progresses, individual PBIs can be added, removed or updated. These changes are immediately visible and help to create a shared vision through a graphical narrative of what the team is trying to achieve.

References

CreativeAgilityTools.com/usm

MoSCoW Your Backlog

Should Have
Could Have
Won't Have
Could Have
Should Have
Must Have

Should Have

A quick prioritization scheme to use when time is tight

When a hard release date is looming and you are concerned about the features that remain to be added, triage your backlog by using MoSCoW analysis. MoSCoW stands for a feature prioritization scheme that divides features into four categories:

- Must have - Features we cannot ship without. If we cut them, we'll fail.
- Should have - Features that can be cut, but would impact us if we do.
- Could have - Features we'd like to keep, but can cut without much impact on the product.
- Won't have - Features we will not keep.

The Practice
Gather the teams (or the product owners on a large product) together and have them go through each epic (major) feature from the product backlog. Choose the epics that will create a "minimum viable product" (MVP) and put them into the "must have" category. Keep in mind that an MVP isn't necessarily a great product, but one that won't fail outright.

Continue going through the remaining epics and discussing if they are "should haves" or "could haves". Having cost and risk estimates for the epics are useful in helping decide this. The features that remain in the first three categories are moved to the "won't have" category.

Tips
- A rough cost estimate for the features will help to prioritize them
- A competitive analysis of other products in the genre or category can also be helpful.
- This practice is useful at the start of release cycles, not just when a deployment is looming.

Related Practices
Risk Prioritization Matrix

Premortems

Identify problems before they happen

A pre-mortem is an imaginary post-mortem held at the start of a product. The participants develop the product, discuss their goals and plan for the product accordingly. Then they put on their "future hats" and imagine themselves gathering a month after the product has been shipped. This is where they describe all the things that went wrong with the product and with their project. These results are used to help identify solutions before problems occur.

The Practice
Small groups of people (5 to 9 in size) gather to create a poster for the product. On this poster, they write the product's goals (genre, market positioning, major features, etc.) and create the plan (critical dates, cost, team structures, etc). Half of the poster is set aside to capture "what went wrong". Teams fill the "what went wrong" section with sticky notes, each containing one area where things went wrong.

After teams complete the above-mentioned steps (30-40 minutes), one person from each team presents their poster to the rest of the group.

Tips
- If there are a lot of "what went wrong" sticky notes on a poster, ask the team to pick the three items that are most impactful to present.
- Identify areas where there are differences in the goals and plan section. This is a great opportunity for a product owner to create a shared vision of what you're making and how you'll be making it.

References
CreativeAgilityTools.com/Premortem

Risk Board

Maintain a board that tracks current major risks

Identifying, tracking and managing risks is critical for developing new products. A Risk Board is a visible "radiator" of the status of each risk.

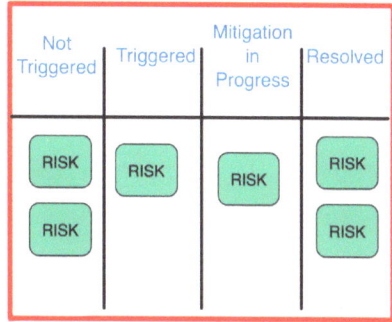

The Practice

A *Risk Board* is a kanban board that tracks *Risk Cards*. Each Risk Card contains the following information:

- Name of the risk
- Priority (see below)
- Trigger – What condition would tell us that the risk has been triggered. This could be a date or a test
- Mitigation – What is the plan for resolving this risk
- Owner – Who is monitoring the trigger or who will own the mitigation if it's triggered

Each product will have a backlog of risks that are refined at least every release. The backlog is prioritized by using T-Shirt Sizing.

The board itself will have four columns representing the four states a risk can be in:

- Untriggered – The highest priority risks we're watching this release
- Triggered – The risks that have hit their trigger condition
- Mitigation in progress – What risks are being mitigated
- Resolved – Risks that we've solved (mitigated or have decided to do nothing about

Tips

- Prioritize risks by t-shirt sizing the impact (cost) of the risk coming true and the likelihood of it coming true. Use the Risk Matrix practice to then sort them into a single list
- Apply WiP limits to the columns so you can manage risks more quickly and evenly

Related Practices

- The Risk Matrix
- T-Shirt Sizing
- Use WiP limits

Shrink Your Backlog

Keep your backlog lean and easy to use

Often times in development the backlog becomes the dumping place of ideas, making it a nightmare to maintain and unusable. One way to solve this problem is to continually reduce the size and complexity of your backlog by turning it into a fun exercise.

The Practice
Instead of dumping ideas in and forgetting about them, strive to keep it lean by:
- Placing ideas into a spreadsheet as soon as they come up
- Keeping the backlog limited to containing features for this current release (2-3 sprints)
- Ensuring that the backlog is reviewed before each sprint planning
- Refining the backlog based on what is learned in an iteration after it has kicked off

Tips
- Just have Features & User Stories in the backlog
- For each release make sure to include release planning that allows your leads get together to clean up and create the new backlog
- Remove items from the backlog as they are added to the product

Spike It!

Create a time-
boxed story to
research
something you
can't yet estimate

Occasionally, there
are stories that can't be estimated because:
- We don't know when something will be "good enough".
- We don't know how to make it work.
- It's the first asset of that type we've made.

Creating an estimate up-front is not only wrong, but it might force a developer to take shortcuts to get something done at a lower quality.

The Practice
Instead of creating a typical story that has a definition of done and an acceptance criteria, create one that outlines the goal of what we're trying to learn and establishes the amount time we are willing to spend on it.

Examples
- "One person spends two weeks porting our product over to the new engine"
- "Artists spend four days tuning the animations to reduce frames"
- "Bill, the designer will continue to tune interactions for the iteration"

T-Shirt Sizing

Get away from arbitrary numbers when sizing your product backlog

For some products, story points are a useful metric for discussing design and forecasting progress. For others, they are a confusing artifact that doesn't help. As a result, some teams have turned to sizing items in their product backlog without points or any other metrics. This is an example of one approach: *T-shirt sizing*.

The Practice

T-shirt sizing requires a team to size items on the backlog by using the "small", "medium" or "large" tag. Teams will start by rank ordering PBIs from the top of the backlog and then divide the list into the three size buckets. Once sized, teams will be able to forecast initial iteration goals by pulling in a certain number of t-shirt sized items. Although t-shirt sizing doesn't use units, teams will often come up with some metric that guides how much of each size into an iteration goal (e. g. medium is twice as big as a small and should require twice the effort).

Tips
- Teams often denote a PBI that is too large for an iteration as a "large", which is a placeholder for needing to break it down further before it is worked on.
- Teams also use outlier sizes XL, XXL, XS to expand the range of sizes.

Related Practices
Rank ordering
Velocity based iteration planning

References
CreativeAgilityTools.com/TShirt

Task Risk Planning

Decide which team is most capable and ready to accept a task

Sometimes you have a task that can be completed by a number of teams or is not urgently needed.

One way to help decide which team is ready to take on the task is the Task Risk Planning strategy that the military uses for mission planning.

The Practice

Risk is broken into two different sets "Task Risks", and "Personnel Risks". Task Risks are things like; Is the feature unknown? Is the technology nonexistent, or new? Is there something similar on the market? Does this fit into the product easily? Personnel Risks are things like; Are people out sick? Do people have the bandwidth required to perform the task? How is their personal life? Do they have the knowledge needed to complete this task?

The risks can then be scored from 1-3, with 1 being a known easy to handle risk and 3 being a scary unknown risk. The score is then added up to see if it is higher than your risk threshold. *The risk threshold should be defined for the entire project.* Once you have this information, you can decide on whether to go ahead or not, or you can move around people/items to lower the risk.

Tips

- This is also a good way to decide if a risky task should even be attempted .
- Some exceptions can be made to the risk threshold.
- Move items around to try and get below the risk threshold.
- When defining your threshold have 3 number ranges, Low, Medium, High Risk.

The Risk Matrix

Prioritize risk so you can resolve it in the best order

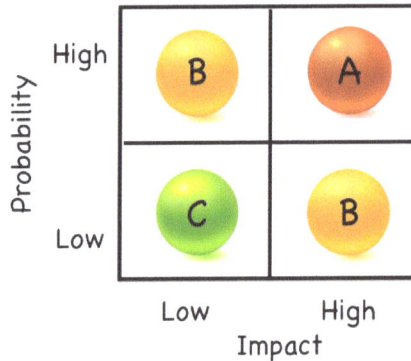

Prioritizing a backlog by cost, value and risk can be challenging as each require different approaches. Prioritizing by risk can be particularly confusing, but there are ways to simplify it.

The Practice
The risk prioritization matrix is simple. Each area of risk that has been identified from a premortem (or other discussion) is placed on a 2x2 map based on the likelihood of the risk manifesting as well as its impact on the product's development. We then prioritize those risks by which quadrant they occupy on the map.

Looking at the matrix above, we prioritize the solutions for risks in the 'A' square first. These could be risks like "we can't find enough good programmers to hire and train in time". Risks in squares 'B' are next. Those risks remaining in square 'C" can be ignored. They are unlikely to manifest and if they do, their impact will probably be minimal.

Tips
You can use rank order to list the risks relative to one another, especially in squares 'B' so that they can be discussed further.

Related Practices
Pre-mortems
Rank ordering

Time Boxing

Get to quality as
quickly as possible

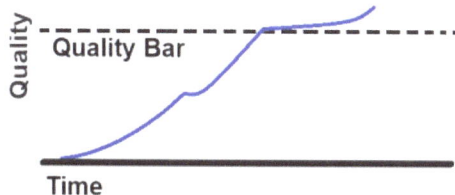

Developers have a desire
to iterate to perfection and
artists in particular are never fully satisfied with their work. So how do
you get them to "great enough" and into the product quickly? Time
boxing is one effective way to do that.

The Practice

- Have your art director set the quality bar and explain how it
  works to your art team. It should also be reinforced during
  dailies.
- When doing time estimates figure out with the artist how long
  it will take them to get to good
- Provide them a little extra time for iteration (example, they
  estimate 3 days, give them 5)
- Explain that they have 5 days to work on the art and no more,
  but once they get to good they can iterate as much as they
  want within that time box.
- You will find that they get to quality much faster when they
  know they have "free time" to iterate. The quality and speed of
  your art will increase.

Tips

- Try to get them to estimate the minimum amount of time it will
  take them to do something, then add 10-20%.
- Keep track of the improvements and make sure to report them
  to your team.
- Always revisit reducing the time boxes through retrospectives
  and measuring cycle time.

Tracer Bullets

Execute vertical slices of features to improve your estimates and identify potential problems

Large (epic) features are difficult to accurately estimate. This is because the estimates are usually based on uncertain dependent areas and humans are pretty bad at estimating a wide range of things. In order to improve our ability to forecast the amount of effort required to do things like creating all the widgets for the product, we can explore a small part of the work, in depth. This is where tracer bullets are useful.

The Practice
A tracer bullet completes a vertical slice of work with the goals of learning more about the cost, risk and value of the whole feature. Using the example of content for the product, here are some potential tracer bullets:
- Create a shippable part of the product with representative uses to extrapolate costs.
- Create a full part of the product that represents the shippable visuals for the product, you can extrapolate art costs.

Once the tracer bullet is executed, the project plan is refined and updated based on what was learned.

Tips
- As the product is refined, repeat tracer bullets every release cycle (2-3 months).
- More than one tracer bullet may be needed to bound a range of a large feature. For example, large interior and large exterior tracer bullets may be useful to identify bounds of cost and technical performance requirements.
- When there's uncertainty regarding what needs to be done, time-boxing can be used to create points to inspect the progress.

Related Practices
Time boxing

Visualize Your Feature Workflow

Make a map of features from concept to deployment and streamline the flow

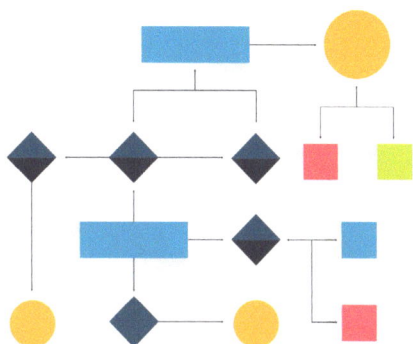

By seeing every step that a feature goes through from concept to deployment in the product, we can start to focus on optimizing the whole flow instead of just the parts, (which lead to waste and delay).

The Practice
Gather a cross-discipline group of people in a room with a large whiteboard and lots of sticky notes. Focusing on their own discipline, have them write down every bit of work that a feature goes through. After 5-10 minutes, have them start posting them on the whiteboard in a flow where the initial idea for the feature is on the top left corner and progresses to the bottom right corner where the feature is in the deployable product. Discuss the flow and improve it by:

- Adding places where a work is waiting around, such as waiting for approval.
- Add an average time that work or waiting takes.
- Add up those times to get your overall cycle time.

The team can then discuss ideas for improving the cycle time or discussing areas of responsibility.

Tips
- Capture the flow with pictures and recreate it using a diagramming tool like Visio or Graffle.
- Use kanban cards to measure the cycle time of features being produced.

Related Practices
Kanban cards
Go SRF-ing

Section 7 - Organizational Improvements

Calendar Refresh

Regularly remove all meetings that no longer serve a purpose

Over time, many recurring meetings build up and people start to forget the original purpose of the meeting. Suddenly, people are attending numerous meetings, many of which seem pointless.

The Practice
- Once a quarter, let everyone know that all meetings will be removed.
- Encourage teams to be sure that meetings they add are required and have a stated purpose.
- Encourage best practices when the meetings are re-added.

Tips
- Double check all meetings that get added back to ensure that they have a purpose.
- Be sure that the minimum number of people are added to meetings.
- Encourage direct communication regarding meetings.
- This practice doesn't excuse the team from assessing the validity of meetings regularly.

Create a Hospitable Place

Make your office environment conducive to good work

It's easy for people who are stressed out or overworked to ignore their surroundings. Poor lighting, acoustics, clutter and random disruptions have an impact on both enjoyment and productivity in the workplace.

The Practice
There is no one practice for creating a more hospitable working environment, but some attention and a small budget can make significant improvements.

Tips
Within an existing space
- Is there a public paging system or other nuisance sound source around you? Shut it off!
- Would artwork or some plants help make your space more attractive and comfortable?
- Is the lighting harsh or glaring? Other fixtures may offer better lighting options.
- Get movable partitions and desks and let the team move them around.

When planning a new space
- Is outdoor lighting important to some team members and not others? We found that programmers like to be near windows, while some artists prefer darker spaces.
- Is it a customizable space or are you forcing teams into cube-ville or completely open floor plans? A mix of both is probably ideal as it gives the team some flexibility to move their desks to create a working environment that is suitable to them.
- Is there enough wall space for tasks and white boards?
- Is there a "pit" or communal area for teams to gather?

Go SRF-ing

Identify people or roles that are needed

Duty	Responsible	Facilitates	Signs-off
Estimates iteration backlog	Developers	Scrum Master	Leads
Updates product backlog	Product Owner	Scrum Master	Publisher
Sets release dates	Publisher	Product Owner	Studio CEO

Over time, responsibilities change. Teams can take on more ownership and responsibilities may shift. Creating a shared agreement about who-does-what for various duties is important so that time is not wasted and nothing critical is missed.

The Practice
Gather a group of people who have various roles and duties together and have them write down (one per sticky note) all of the duties that are needed to get work done. Create a matrix on a large white board with four columns. Duties will go into the left-most column. The other three columns will list how these duties map to roles based on the following criteria:
- **Signs-off** - This is the role that will approve or reject the result of the duty
- **Responsible** - This is who will actually do the work described by the duty
- **Facilitates** - This is who will ensure that the practices are supporting the duty is being fulfilled

The group will then discuss the roles that fill the matrix for each duty (see example).

Example
In the chart above, the developers are responsible for estimating the work they can accomplish in an iteration. The Scrum Master will facilitate the estimation, but the lead will sign-off on those estimates.

Tips
- You can expand the columns to include those who must be informed or consulted, etc.
- The output from the 'visual display of your feature workflow' can be used to identify the duties

Related Practices
Visual display of your feature workflow

Office Phone Booth

A small phone booth in open work spaces where people can make private phone calls

The Practice
If your open office doesn't have (enough) private, convenient spaces for phone conversations, you can buy a stand-alone phone booth. These typically take up a square meter of floor space and are built to be relatively sound-proof.

References
An example phone booth for sale:
CreativeAgilityTools.com/PhoneBooth

Propaganda Poster

Turn pillars into visible posters

It's important to build out your vision using key pillars and a key phrase. Even if they are written down, if they are not in the forefront of everyone's mind during development, they won't get referenced and become devalued. One way to turn those items into exciting reminders is to turn them into propaganda posters and hang them around the office.

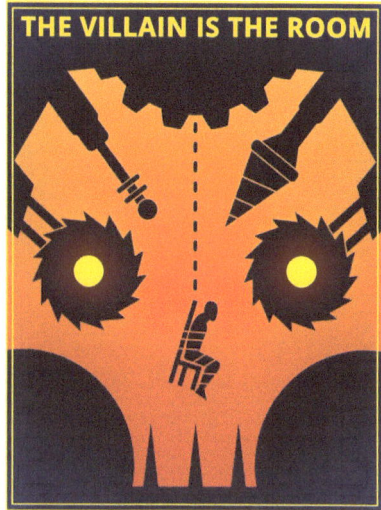

THE VILLAIN IS THE ROOM

Image courtesy of Chuck Hoover and Schell Games

The Practice
- Identify your pillars and key phrases.
- Have artists on the team build a propaganda poster that shows off those pillars and phrases.
- Once you have designed and agreed on the poster, have copies printed and place them where the team will see them often.

Tips
Having them around the team area makes sure they are referenced regularly.

Related Practices
Love Card Wall

Retrospect Your Company

Facilitate a company-wide conversation on getting better

Companies need a retrospective every once in a while, to improve. An excellent practice for doing this is called "Open Space".

The Practice
Open Space is usually a half or full day gathering where groups iterate through one-hour cycles. A cycle consists of a gathering of attendees creating breakout topics. The breakouts follow for 30 minutes and then the participants regroup to hear a summary of what was discussed during the breakout sessions.

What makes Open Space unique is its open nature. Allowing everyone to move around freely between breakouts gives rise to unhampered creativity that can result in new ideas that might have otherwise been overlooked. For example, a group once asked if a cook could be hired to prepare breakfasts and this suggestion was implemented - it demonstrates a unique way to increase productivity)! Another group discussed improvements to the art pipeline which went on to attract dozens of people and resulted in major improvements to the shared pipeline.

Tips
- Breakouts will often generate follow-up action items. Make sure there is someone who will be responsible for the follows-up (often the person who created the topic).
- Don't make it mandatory. Although you are giving a voice to everyone in the company, some won't want to participate. Don't force them to. If your company finds value in Open Space, they will probably join in the future.

References
CreativeAgilityTools.com/OpenSpace

Team Space Design

Give teams a budget to refine their own work area

There is endless debate about whether open space, cube farm or individual office layouts are the best. Each layout has its own benefits and drawbacks and a 'one-size-fits-all' approach is never ideal. One solution is to let the teams decide on their own what will make them most comfortable and give them the budget to implement changes and make adjustments to their space accordingly.

The Practice
Create a budget that allows for teams to spend what is required to upgrade their spaces. Let them decide, within constraints, how to layout and upgrade their space.

Tips
- Tie this into agility. Connect upgrades to iteration retrospective actions instead of a few times a year.
- Have teams prioritize space upgrades and evaluate, among all teams, the relative need among them all to determine which team to fund first. Use the "buy a feature" practice to do this.
- Consider limiting or encouraging furniture purchases to mobile and reconfigurable options. Examples are work desks on casters and desks that can be raised or lowered for standing/sitting options.
- Clearly define things the team can't do themselves that would require outside help such as moving heavy furniture or running electrical conduits. (Seriously. We had a team run live 120-volt lines).
- Create a market for second hand furniture that other teams have elected to no longer use.
- Have a facility "point person" that the team can coordinate with regarding requests.
- Try to avoid "budget competitions" by setting budget amounts that have to be spent every year or lost (or reduced).

Related Practices
Buy a Feature

Use a Remote Meeting Space

An off-site meeting place allows for discussions without interruptions and distractions

Occasionally teams, leads or discipline groups need a large chunk of time to focus together on solving a problem or planning something out in detail. Doing this in the workplace can be challenging **because:**
- It might be hard to reserve a space for the day.
- There are constant interruptions.
- The temptation to "check in" on the product or coworkers is a distraction.

The Practice
The practice is to rent an offsite meeting space.

Tips
- Have one point of contact for emergencies and ask attendees to put their devices aside.
- Set established "communication breaks" for people to check in with the company.
- Avoid renting their equipment (like projectors, screens and flip charts). Hotels often charge more than the cost of buying the equipment outright!
- Find a place where you can visit local restaurants at lunch. This has the benefit of getting out of the space for a break and avoiding high-priced catering.
- More and more companies, like breather.com, are offering meeting spaces that can be managed entirely on the internet.

Note
This building is located in a remote part of Iceland where game industry leaders met in 2017. It was an ideal location for focusing on our work.

Section 8 - Team Culture

360 Reviews

Have teams review their peers frequently and regularly

Have teams review themselves more frequently and on a regular basis. One way to do this is through 360 reviews. These reviews are dramatically more impactful than yearly performance reviews. They provide direct feedback from peers and happen often enough to engender improvements.

The Practice

At least once every three months, have each member of a team (less than 10 people) review the other team members. The typical review format is to rate others on a simple scale of one (needs improvement), to five (is a strength) on characteristics such as collaboration, technical skills, leadership, initiative, etc. The results are gathered, averaged and handed out. Often, the results are reviewed with a discipline lead to discuss and compare with previous results.

Tips

- Avoid doing them by hand as they are time consuming. There are great software packages for conducting 360 reviews through a web page.
- Having a field for gathering comments can be useful but comments often have to be reviewed and filtered manually and therefore take up valuable time.
- Avoid collecting and sharing comments for newly formed teams until they've had time to settle in and work with one another for at least a month.

References

CreativeAgilityTools.com/360

20% Time

Set aside some time to
explore   and re-focus

There are many names and
variations for this practice, such
as Google time, FedEx days,
demo days, etc. There are
various examples of
implementations, but the basic
idea is the same.

The Practice
20% of development time is reserved for exploring an idea that
developers come up with on their own. This should be a time where
there are minimal constraints in terms of what is produced.

Examples of Constraints
- Must be able to demo the work
- The demo must meet a definition of done (e.g. runs on an
  iPhone)
- The result must be something that can be used in a product

Examples of Implementations
- Amnesia Fortnight: Forget about the current project and
  develop something in 2 weeks that can be used to pitch for an
  actual product.
- FedEx days: Create something that must be delivered in 24
  hours

References
CreativeAgilityTools.com/20Percent

Ask Powerful Questions

Ask questions that drive thoughtful answers

Powerful questions are questions which are impactful and drive thought and conversation. They also avoid evasive or short responses.

The Practice
Asking powerful questions takes practice and the following basic rules can help you get the results you are looking for:
- Keep questions short.
- Avoid questions that have a yes or no answer.
- Don't ask rhetorical questions.
- Use the **silent count to 10** practice waiting for answers. They require thought.

Examples:
- What is hindering us from reaching the iteration goal?
- What are you enjoying about the product right now?
- What do you feel about the product we are making?
- If you could fix one thing about the way we work, what would it be?
- How else could you have solved that problem?

Related Practices
The Silent Count

Demo
Iteration

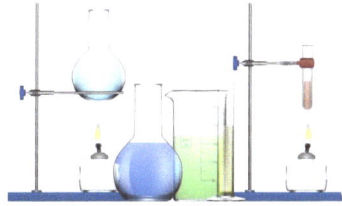

Energize a team by letting
them have some fun on their own

Sometimes a team's creative focus can become too narrow and this
can impact their productivity. Taking a week or two off to explore and
develop an unplanned mechanic can recharge them and even
generate some valuable ideas.

The Practice
Ask a group of people to form teams for a single iteration's effort to
create an unplanned mechanic for the product. Communicate the
goals of the iteration (see tips below) and leave them alone for the
duration. At the end of the iteration, hold a demo of each new
mechanic.

Tips
- Have a few constraints for the team that helps guide them
  towards a goal:
    - Define the work. Include performance, quality and
      platform definitions.
    - Communicate a vision. For example, Double Fine
      established a vision of creating demos that could be
      sold as a prototype for a full game. All four of their first
      "Amnesia Fortnight" demos were signed for full
      games.
    - Ask for a pitch. One to two weeks of downtime is
      expensive. Have teams form and propose an idea
      using a given template before you approve their demo
      iteration. Use chartering ideas such as "product box"
      instead of documents. A benefit of this practice is to
      allow teams to experiment with self-organization, so
      don't manage their efforts.
- Have a review with the entire company or group to demo and
  celebrate what was accomplished!

References
CreativeAgilityTools.com/DemoIteration

Related Practices
Product Box

Effective Postmortems

Diagnose issues that have emerged and provide a clear plan to fix them

Postmortems are often not very effective as people tend to gather in a room and complain about what went wrong. Some may even take notes and there is a consensus that "we won't do that next time", but follow through is often lacking and the same mistakes continue to be made. Postmortems can be more useful if they are used not as the end point but as the midpoint, similar to the half times in sports. A team can be trailing when they go into a halftime and come out of it fired up enough to go on to win the game.

The Practice
Postmortems should be done regularly and preferably at the end of each iteration to see what you can improve on before going into the next iteration. It is important to focus' first on what went right, then on what went wrong. Open up the floor and have people just shout out what they thought went right/wrong. After doing that for a few minutes focus on each list. Have the room work together to identify the top 3 things in each group. Then spend some time discussing what specifically can be done to fix what went wrong. You should make sure to take good notes on every topic that is brought up. After the meeting is over have the team leadership meet to discuss the top 3 things that went wrong and the suggested fixes. Solidify plans for how you will go about fixing them as a team. Then message out to the whole team the notes from the meeting with the action items for fixing the top 3 items at the top of that message. Then in your iteration kickoff cover them again.

Tips
- Make sure your postmortem doesn't turn into a circle of complaining, keep it directed.
- Make sure people don't point the finger at each other.

Related Practices
Premortems

Elephant in the Room

Identify the biggest problem quickly and address it

Often there are topics that seem better left alone, but not discussing them can really hurt the project or team. One of the most important jobs of a leader is addressing these items swiftly and carefully.

The Practice
- The first step is to bring up the issue with the correct group, gently and respectfully.
- Make sure to focus on the issue and not the individuals involved.
- Ask appropriate questions with sensitivity to bring more awareness and understanding about the issue to everyone involved. This also helps to normalize the topic in conversation.
- Identify the next steps and make sure the actions are clear to everyone involved.

Tips
- Follow up with each individual separately to ensure that they are on the same page.
- Check in regularly to see that action items are being worked on effectively and efficiently.

References
CreativeAgilityTools.com/Elephant

Free Day/Free Week

Reward hard work with creative time

One way to reward the team for their hard work is to give them a free day once a month, or even an entire week after a big milestone. This is a great way to get new ideas for the product, lower stress, have the team work with different people, and build team unity.

The Practice
Take one day a month and allow individuals to work on anything they want in relation to the product, it may be anything from tools to a crazy new mode. Make sure to timebox them to only work on it during their free day, or in their own time (it may take multiple free days). Then in the next team meeting allow people to show off what they have made in a short little video.

The free week is a great way to have individuals work with different people on the project that they might not work with normally. Tell the team that after the next milestone they will get a week to work on any feature they might want to add to the product or prototype. Make sure they know it must have a deliverable within that week and that finishing it doesn't guarantee it will make it into the product. The following week have a team meeting and let everyone show off what they made!

Tips
- Do provide some guidance to make sure they aren't going totally off the rails.
- Be aware that some things that are created may be well loved but may just not make it into the product. If this does happen, take the time to explain to the team why it is a great feature and why it won't work in the product you are making.

Related Practices
20% Time

Group Confession

Encourage the team to be more open, less proud and more willing to learn from fails

It's important to allow a safe place for people to learn from each other's mistakes and how to handle them when they arise. This practice is for helping create that place.

The Practice
Once a month have the team meet in an informal space and allow everyone to "confess" some mistakes that they have made in the last month. Have them explain what they did wrong and how they either fixed it or tried to fix it. This isn't supposed to be a place to judge but to discuss and learn. This helps a lot with openness, trust and creating that "safe to fail" culture. One of the best things it helps with though is making the more proud team members swallow their pride and admit to failing.

Tips
- Keep the mood light and fun.
- Make sure everyone has at least one story to share.
- The story doesn't have to be from the last month, but it helps if it is from the same project.
- Try to meet in a less formal space than a meeting room.
- Try the "failure bow", which is a deep bow following a confession, especially when done spontaneously, that will also lighten the mood.

Lighten the Mood

Don't punish people
for making mistakes -
It's how we often learn

Some cultures don't
tolerate mistakes very well
and when someone makes a mistake they can become a target for
blame. This can result in a fear of making mistakes which in turn can
stifle learning and innovation. People end up "playing it safe" and only
do what they are told to and if they do make a mistake, they try to hide
it.

The Practice
Communicating that making mistakes is part of the process when
developing products (as well as being a human), is important. There
are several things that companies, and teams have done to "lighten
the mood" when someone makes a mistake. In fact, one company
gave a small trophy to the developer who made the biggest mistake
every iteration or two. This *"Biggest goof-up award"* was handed out,
with honorable mentioned to runners-up to thunderous applause.

Various reward approaches have been used for developers who
"break the build" after a commit, bringing the entire Product staff to a
grinding halt. Examples include:
- A Muppet singing on all the developers PC's with a popup
  announcing the offender's name.
- A token placed at the offender's workstation until another
  developer breaks the build (we used a loaf of bread that
  became increasingly moldy over time).
- One company had a life-sized cut-out of Justin Bieber. When
  someone broke the build for the first time, Justin stood beside
  their desk; the second time, he was on their desk and the third
  time he went with them wherever they went.

Tips
These "awards" or policies are never meant to be humiliating. I've
seen some of them used with teams that were not getting along very
well and the humor was lost, so use this method with care.

Love Card Wall

Build team culture by sharing moments of respect and appreciation visually

The Practice
Team members identify moments of appreciation, goodwill, and respect throughout the iteration by writing a brief note of what happened on a sticky note. The notes are posted in a team open space, (possibly the war room) for all to see.

Tips
- You can find heart-shaped sticky notes for sale online
- Anyone can write a love card for any instance they encounter, even if it's between two co-workers
- The coach (or Scrum Master) will encourage these to be written throughout the iteration

Related Practices
War room
Notes of Encouragement

No Meeting Days

Provide a regular day to focus on desk work

It happens to all of us - your calendar is filled with meetings all day and you don't have the time to get your daily work completed. Sure meetings are work, but they don't take the place of the work you were scheduled to accomplish. Since meetings, as effective as they may be, can block work from getting done, it is a good idea to provide a day (weekly if you can) where no meetings are scheduled.

The Practice
- Select a day with the leads, producers/PO that works best for your team.
- Inform the team that there won't be meetings on the day selected (other days may have more).
- Make sure there is an understanding to not schedule meetings on those days.

Tips
- Regularly remind the meeting schedulers of this rule.
- Block off people's schedules so no one outside of the team can book meetings for that day.
- Check regularly to see if a different day might work better.

Related Practices
Silent Hour

Notes of Encouragement

Encourage and reward awesome work with a personal touch

When someone does something awesome it's valuable to bring attention to what they have done, but sometimes it is more meaningful (and depending on their personality type more desirable) to be thanked quietly with a note.

The Practice
- Get some simple (but colorful) 3x5 cards and a pen or marker.
- Identify the person you want to thank/encourage and write a personal heartfelt message.
- Leave it on their desk when they aren't around so they can come back to it.

Tips
- Don't limit these notes to just the people doing big awesome things - include notes for people doing simple but necessary work.
- Aim to write at least one note a week.
- Get creative and decorate the cards.

Related Practices
Love Card Wall

References
Book: "How Full is your Bucket" – Tom Rath & Donald Clifton

Open Topic Board

Get feedback and generate ideas as a team

Sometimes it's good to open up aspects of the product or the project itself to get feedback and ideas from everyone on the project. One way to do this is to have an open topic board where people can add their ideas or thoughts and upvote them for visibility.

The Practice
Set up a board, either magnetic or cork, in a central location. Once every few weeks add a new highlighted topic to the top of the board, making sure it has a clear start and end date. Provide cards and markers for people to write down their ideas. Encourage the team to read each card and add a mark to upvote them. Once the time period is up, have the person who posted the topic review the feedback and ideas that were received and share any decisions that were made as a result at the next team meeting.

Tips
- Make sure you monitor what people are putting on the board to make sure they are on topic.
- When reviewing the topics in the team meeting make sure to address the top upvoted item even if you aren't going to use it and explain the reasons why it will or won't work.
- This is not an ideal practice to use if your team isn't trusting of each other or aren't on board with the vision for the product.
- You can use this for everything from generating widget ideas to determining what to have stocked in the kitchen.

Pecha Kucha Introductions

Help build a team by learning about each other

Pecha Kucha

10 X 10

When forming a new team there are many ways to assist people in bonding quickly. One of the quickest ways is by gaining a shared understanding of each other and focusing on commonalities. A great way to do that is through personal Pecha Kucha Introductions.

The Practice

As a fun exercise (not a homework assignment), have each person create a slideshow about themselves that consists of:

- 10 Slides per person
- 10 Seconds per slide (auto advance)
- Nothing about their professional life (except schooling) and what inspired them to make products

Then have a fun event with food and drinks where everyone has a chance to go through their slideshow. The goal is to encourage cohesion by getting people to learn about similarities they share or interesting facts about each other.

Tips

- If your team is larger than 10 people, consider having multiple meetings.
- Create a slide deck/template with the auto advancing rules in Google Slides, PowerPoint or Keynote and have people contribute to them.
- You can also do this informally using index cards.
- Set aside a time for people to work on their slideshow during work
- It's important to show only pictures. No text.

References
CreativeAgilityTools.com/PechaKucha

Prototype Team

Allow the team to be adventurous and explore new possibilities

One way to keep a live project
exciting and fresh is to have a team that is constantly working on prototypes. This team can either be the one coming up with the prototypes, or they can be fed ideas from other sources.

The Practice
Have a team that is responsible for taking a new idea each iteration (or less) and making a prototype out of it in a contained space (branch). Allow anyone to make suggestions to the team and have them approved by the leadership before the work begins. Make sure that the teams have plenty of freedom when they work and cycle team members regularly to keep people on the project fresh and creative.

Tips
- Make sure the team knows that the prototypes may not make it into the product at any point.
- Consider this to be a 'pressure valve' for the project and individuals.
- Cycle people on the team every few months.
- Make sure they are supported and can easily access what they need from outside the team.

Silent Hour

A solid uninterrupted hour of work

We are constantly interrupted while working, this can have a lot of negative side effects especially for programmers. But collaboration and communication are vital parts of product creation, so you don't want to ruin that. But what if 1 hour a day was dedicated to just working alone at your desk?

The Practice
- Set aside one hour every day that is for work time alone.
- During that time have everyone shut off emails and any other digital communication devices.
- Make sure people know that the hour has started.
- Encourage people to wear headphones.
- If your offices have doors, shut them.

Tips
- It's important that everyone at the company participate or at least respect the teams that are participating, so make sure everyone is aware of the silent hour.
- Obviously urgent things do come up, so make sure you have at a least producer/PO who is still monitoring communicate lines in case something needs to be escalated.

Related Practices
No Meetings Day

Socialize the Team

Build team unity through social interactions

Building a new team can be challenging and adding team members can also be a challenge. One of the easiest ways to improve how teams work together is by helping them to get to know each other better. One easy way to accomplish this without making it feeling like a "trust fall" exercise is to encourage the team to socialize both at work and outside the office.

The Practice
- This practice is simple. Come up with fun things that the team can do that will allow them to socialize often.
- Ideas for in the office:
    - Birthday celebrations, for big companies once a month
    - Holiday celebrations
    - Team happy hour
    - Game time, play board games together
    - Team dinners
- Ideas for outside of the office
    - Laser tag
    - Go karts
    - Whirlyball
    - Rent out an arcade, have food and drinks
    - Picnics
    - Museum outings
    - Sports outings
    - Dinners
    - Mini Olympics
    - Bowling

Tips
- These events should be scheduled during office hours.
- These events must be company sponsored.
- If you offer alcohol at any event, make sure they have a safe option to get home.
- Make sure your leadership team is present and participates in these events.
- To discourage clicks, find ways for the team to mix with new people at these events.
- Select events that encourage collaboration and competition.

110

Space for Retrospectives

Let the developers retrospect before bringing in a loud product owner

Having a product owner attend the team's retrospective is valuable, but if the product owner's voice is louder than the rest of the team, it can silence the more quiet members of the team.

The Practice

The developers start the retrospective by reviewing all of the events that impacted them during the iteration and generate insights into possible root causes. The product owner is then invited into the meeting so that the results can be shared with them and decisions can be made regarding whether any practices need to start, stop, or continue in order to reach their goals successfully.

Tips
- Establish a time-box for the developer-only retrospective so the product owner can schedule.
- The goal should be for the product owner to attend the entire retrospective. Let the product owner know that (for now) the meetings will include discussion time with team before the product owner arrives to ensure that everyone has a chance to voice their opinions.
- Use this time to activate "The Quiet Ones" - those team members, who were unlikely to speak when product owner was present.
- If the product owner is also developing with the team they need to attend the entire retrospective without dominating the discussion.

Team Hardening Week

A week of daily iterations designed to help the team increases quality, alignment and vision

At the end of feature development or a prototype, we give the team a week to "harden" the product. This includes exploring and balancing systems, discussing the product's direction and ways to create universal buy-in.

The Practice
The week consists of five daily iterations. Each iteration consists of:
1. A mandatory one-hour use session for the entire team. Everyone on the team provides observations on areas that need fixing, polishing and fine tuning.
2. The observations are taken into account and a plan for the day is created.
3. The team implements as much of this plan as they can.
4. A new build is created.

Tips
- Create a safe space for the team - nothing is more sacred!
- This works best with small prototype/pre-production teams. It helps by:
    - Aligning everyone to the vision of the product
    - Encouraging the team to experiment knowing that even after spending a day trying something out it can be abandoned with no regret if it doesn't show promise.

Team Health

Quickly identify your project's health through team health

The best way to determine the health of your project is by knowing the health of each of the working teams. When discussing your team's health and progress at a high level, it's best to have a common language and quick visual way to review all the teams.

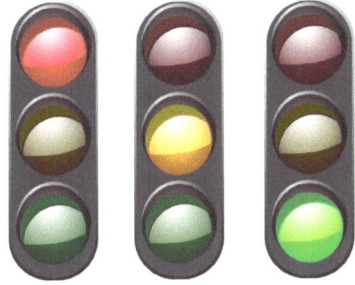

The Practice
Create a spreadsheet, or board with each team listed by name with a space to include a color-coded cell/card. Each time your Scrum Masters meet (scrum of scrums) have them update each of their team's health indicators.

- **Red** - Something is wrong and it should be addressed immediately (examples: blocked, team member is sick, internal dysfunction)
- **Yellow** - The team is getting work done but might be running into some small problems. These should be monitored and addressed when possible (examples: off-team communication, requests are being missed)
- **Green** - The team is progressing well on their iteration and are in good overall health

Tips
Have the SM regularly ask team members questions to assess how the team members feel things are.

Related Practices
A Fourth Daily Question

References
CreativeAgilityTools.com/TeamHealth

The 5 Whys

A retrospective technique for getting to the root cause of a problem

Retrospectives are an essential part of creating a cycle of continuous improvement. Often, it is hard to come up with specific solutions that can be implemented right away. The **5 whys** practice can help teams focus on actionable solutions. A retrospective starts with a ideation phase where the issues and impediments encountered over the previous iteration are collected. The second phase involves generating insights into why these problems occurred. Often, the root cause of a problem is several layers deep and must be dug out. The 5 whys is an effective practice for accomplishing this.

The Practice
Divide the team up into small groups of 2-4 people. For each problem, have one person ask the other(s) "Why did this problem occur?". For each answer ask "why" again. After no more than five answers, you should arrive at the root cause of the problem which lends itself to a solution. The root cause is recorded and the group moves on to the next question. When the groups reconvene, the root causes are discussed and solutions are generated in the next phase of the retrospective.

Example
- "We waste a lot of time every morning."
- "Why?"
- "The build is always broken in the morning."
- "Why?"
- "Commits are made late during the previous day that are not sufficiently tested."
- "Why"
- "There are no target machines to test on at the end of the day."
- "Why"
- "QA does all their regression testing at the end of the day."

At this point, you may be at a root cause that can be addressed, such as if QA can do their regression testing at a different time of the day or if additional target hardware can be purchased.

Use the Koosh Ball

A simple token for conversation among a large group of people

The Practice
The practice of going around a circle of people to answer a question can create anxiety or a lack of engagement among the group. A more random or voluntary way of gathering feedback is by using a **Koosh ball**.

The Practice
A Koosh ball is a very soft device that can be cheaply purchased in many places. The basic rule is that the only person allowed to speak is the one holding the Koosh ball. When that person is done speaking, they can toss the Koosh ball to someone who signals they want to speak, by holding their hand up. Alternatively, the speaker can toss the ball to anyone else in the group as long as they can make eye contact before the throw. This continues until a time box is complete or conversation dies down.

Tips
- Announce the rules at the start.
- The facilitator may reserve the right to speak in the event someone breaks the rules or is hogging the Kush.
- If you need to pick up conversation, ask powerful questions.

Related Practices
Ask Powerful Questions

Wall of Pain

Capture painful processes/
bottlenecks/errors that are
current, even if they can't
be fixed immediately

Sometimes it's hard to remember
all the little blockers that impact
you on a daily basis. This
practice helps you capture them
so they are not forgotten and if
they bother enough people, raise the urgency of a solution.

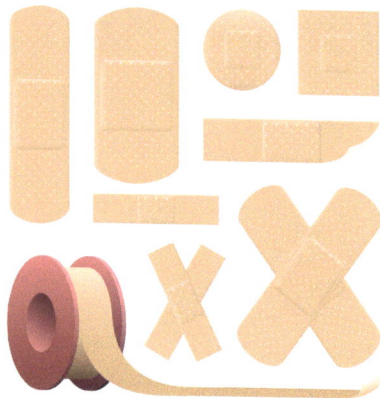

The Practice

The practice is simple: capture short descriptions or reminders of a
problem as they occur (pain cards) and post them where they can be
seen by the rest of the team. As people encounter problems, they can
add additional pain cards or dot vote one that is already there. During
the next planning session, pain cards with the most votes (through dot
voting or roman voting) can have solutions placed on the iteration
backlog.

Tips

- Pain cards can be physical, in a war room, or virtual in a wiki.
- Problems can also be written on story cards, if they have an
  impact on that story

Related Practices

War room
Dot voting
Roman voting
Health check

Further Reading

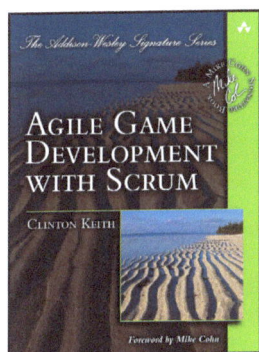

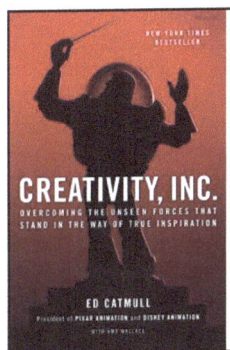

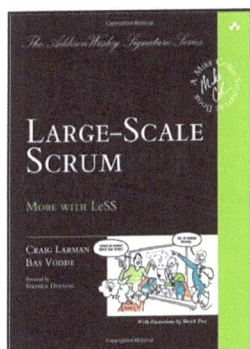

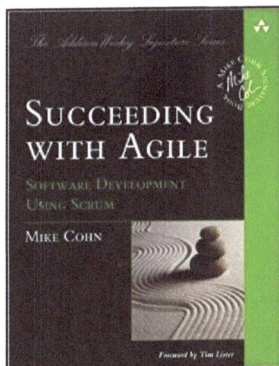

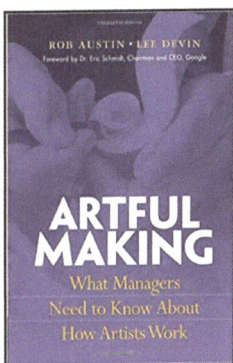

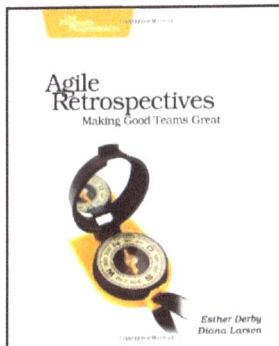

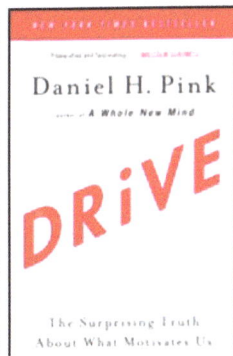

Agile Game Development with Scrum
The Addison-Wesley Signature Series
Clinton Keith
Foreword by Mike Cohn

Lean from the Trenches
Managing Large-Scale Projects with Kanban
Henrik Kniberg
Foreword by Kent Beck

Creativity, Inc.
NEW YORK TIMES BESTSELLER
Overcoming the Unseen Forces That Stand in the Way of True Inspiration
Ed Catmull
President of Pixar Animation and Disney Animation
With Amy Wallace

Large-Scale Scrum
The Addison-Wesley Signature Series
More with LeSS
Craig Larman
Bas Vodde

Succeeding with Agile
The Addison-Wesley Signature Series
Software Development Using Scrum
Mike Cohn
Foreword by Tim Lister

Artful Making
Rob Austin · Lee Devin
Foreword by Dr. Eric Schmidt, Chairman and CEO, Google
What Managers Need to Know About How Artists Work

User Story Mapping
O'REILLY
Discover the Whole Story, Build the Right Product
Jeff Patton
with Peter Economy
Forewords by Martin Fowler, Alan Cooper, and Marty Cagan

Agile Retrospectives
Making Good Teams Great
Esther Derby
Diana Larsen

Drive
Daniel H. Pink
author of A Whole New Mind
The Surprising Truth About What Motivates Us

Practice Credits

This book was a community effort. Below are the names of the authors of the practices listed by the number of practices they contributed.

Clinton Keith
20% Time
360 Reviews
Actively Listen
Add a Fourth Daily Question
Art Verification Column
Ask Powerful Questions
Automate QA
Beachhead a New Practice
Blessed Build Indicator
Build SMART Goals
Burndown your PBIs
Buy a Feature
Create a Hospitable Place
Demo Iteration
Dot Voting
Embrace Risk
Estimate in Days not Hours
Feature Flow Cards
Fishbone a Problem
Form a Stability Team
Form Guilds
Product Box
Go SFR-ing
GROW the Future
Initiation Project
Kanban Cards
Kano your Backlog
LeSS Roles
Lighten the Mood
Map your Stories
MoSCoW Your Backlog
Multi-Team Sprint
Office Phone Booth
Pair Problem Solve
Planning Poker
Premortems
Rank Ordering
Reduce Integration Time
Rename Scrum Terms
Retrospect Your Company
Risk Board

Roman Voting
Scrumble!
The Silent Count
Spike It!
Sprint Day
Swim Lanes
T-Shirt Sizing
Table Challenge
Talk to the Board
Team Space Design
The "Done Done" Column
The 5 Whys
The Build Health Radiator
The Build Monkey
The Review Bazaar
The Risk Matrix
Tracer Bullets
Track Emergent Work
Use a Remote Meeting Space
Use the Koosh Ball
Use WiP Limits
Visualize Your Feature Workflow
War Room
Wednesday Pizza Topic
WiP Tokens
World Café

Grant Shonkwiler
Bug Bash
Calendar Refresh
Define Product Pillars
Effective Postmortems
Elephant In the Room
Fix Bugs Now
Free Day/Free Week
Group Confession
Individual Health
Iteration Reviews
No Meeting Days
Notes of Encouragement
Open Topic Board
PechaKucha Introductions

Prototype Team
Shrink Your Backlog
Silent Hour
Socialize the Team
Task Risk Planning
Team Health
Time Boxing

GDC Contributors (anonymous)
LEGO Tracking
Viking Point

Scott Crabtree
PechaKucha Introductions

Andy Pickett
Wall of Pain

Dagbjort Jonsdottir
Buddy System

Chuck Hoover & Grant Shonkwiler
Propaganda Poster

Jon Lawrence
Start Meetings Efficiently

Mantin Lu
Love Card Wall

Marcin Kruczkiewicz
Space for Retrospectives

Marie-Renee Brisebois
Fix-it Friday

Max Krembs & Andrew Curley
Priority Status Board

Roman Graebsch
Team Hardening Week

Tatu Teittinen
Struggle Ducky

Vladimir Savelyev
Cross Interview

www.ingramcontent.com/pod-product-compliance
Lightning Source LLC
Chambersburg PA
CBHW041710200326
41518CB00001B/139